The Cows Are Out!

Two Decades on a Maine Dairy Farm

The Cows Are Out!

Two Decades on a Maine Dairy Farm

Trudy Chambers Price

ISLANDPORT PRESS
YARMOUTH • FRENCHBORO • MAINE

Islandport Press Inc.
P.O. Box 10
Yarmouth, Maine 04096
islandport@islandportpress.com
www.islandportpress.com

ISBN: 0-9671662-9-2
Library of Congress Control Number: 2003116211

First Edition Published April 2004
Second Edition Published October 2004

Book design by Islandport Press Inc.
Cover design by Karen F. Hoots / Mad Hooter Design
Cover photo of Kyle and Travis Price by Trudy Chambers Price
Interior photos courtesy of Trudy Price unless otherwise noted

To farm women everywhere,
with special thanks to Katie Johnson

Time Capsule

The other day
I watched my grown son
mowing hay.

From a distance
the tractor looked small enough
to be a toy.

And it seemed as though
the man should be a boy.

Trudy Chambers Price

Illustration by Gordon Hammond
Originally published in Echoes: Rediscovering Community (1990)

Acknowledgments

I have worked in the book business since I left dairy farming fifteen years ago. Along the way, I have met many writers and published authors. I don't know of any who write successfully alone. When I first began my writing marathon I was desperate for help because I needed to know if my stories were any good. Yes, I could fill two pages with the names of family, friends, and members of writing groups who in some way helped me get these stories between real covers — they know who they are (and some are now deceased). I decided to celebrate and say thank you again, in person, if possible, to all of them. But in the end, I want to thank, in writing, Dean Lunt, my editor. Dean grew up in a Maine fishing family, so he understood my subject and the meaning of Maine roots. He saw potential in my stories. He challenged me to cut, expand and stretch. He listened patiently and responded to my ideas, honored my input, gave me options, choices and encouragement. When he asked me to write an epilogue, I didn't think I could. It was too emotional. He waited. Eventually, I poured out a stream of consciousness while tears dripped on my keyboard. I sent it to him. Dean helped me include those thoughts in an appropriate and sensitive way.

Thank you, Dean.

Contents

Foreword

In *The Cows Are Out!*, Trudy Price takes us through twenty-three years of family life on her dairy farm in Knox, Maine. Starting in 1966, she describes in entertaining and intimate detail both the joys and struggles of raising two boys and of trying to run a medium-sized farm. Craneland Farm as run by her and her husband, Ron, was noted for its herd of registered Holsteins and its milk production output. The Price family was recognized as Maine Dairy Farm Family of the Year in 1981 for its modern dairy practices, as well as its involvement in community and farm organizations. Such achievements are not easy, nor do they guarantee financial success. Starting a dairy enterprise and keeping up with new technology requires considerable debt. The family worked from sunup to sundown just to keep their heads above water. In the beginning, Trudy even had to leave full-time farm work to teach elementary school so the family could buy new equipment and pay the bills. The family's trials and tribulations to stay competitive as other farms dropped by the wayside during this period is an intriguing story. Trudy humanizes an industry in crisis and celebrates a culture and way of life that is threatened.

Maine's dairy industry has come a long way since the mid-1960s when the Price family took over Craneland Farm. Back then, it took more than two cows to produce what one does today. Although the number of commercial farms has dropped considerably, total milk production has held relatively steady after peaking in the early sixties. Production set a new high in 1999 at nearly 80 million gallons, before dropping to 75 million gallons in 2002. About 45 percent of Maine milk is shipped out of state. It has also been an era of consolidation. In 1965, 2,050 dairy farms operated in Maine. Today, there are less than 400. The number has fallen from 655 just since 1989. Consider these numbers:

Year	Farms	Cows
1950	4,950	109,000
1960	3,250	112,000
1970	1,900	69,000
1980	1,065	57,000
1990	672	42,000
2000	466	40,000
2003	395	35,000 (est.)

These are relevant and important statistics. The Maine dairy farm provides more than just beautiful scenery and desirable land use; it is a critical economic staple for rural Maine and the cornerstone of the state's agricultural economy. The industry provides more than one hundred million dollars annually in milk, cattle, and crop sales, and helps maintain the infrastructure upon which all Maine farms depend.

Currently, the industry faces unprecedented challenges. The loss of dairy farms is alarming. With milk prices well below the cost of production, more than one hundred Maine dairy farms left the dairy industry in the past three years alone. Another ninety-eight are expected to leave the industry in five years due to operator retirement. Farms today basically operate in a crisis situation, with the price of milk paid to farmers at twenty-year lows. Maine dairy farmers have been forced to sell milk for $1.05 per gallon, when the short-run, break-even price to cover operating and overhead costs is $1.36 to produce it.* Larger farms fared much better, with $1.13 for their short-run,

*The cost of production is based on the 2002 Dairy Cost of Production Survey conducted by the University of Maine.

break-even price. The trend has been toward fewer and larger farms over the years. For many, the debt load is untenable, forcing many farmers to sell, and the farms to be turned into housing developments, which exacerbates urban sprawl.

It is not just dairy farms that are impacted by low milk prices. There is a ripple effect on other industry-related jobs, such as hired help on the farm; milk haulers and processors; feed, seed, and fertilizer suppliers; equipment dealers; veterinarians; bank lenders; and a host of farm-related fieldmen and suppliers.

It is primarily our dairy farmers that utilize open space and sustain our rural communities as desirable places to live and work. The rolling hills with grazing cows and working farms represent the very heart of Maine's character. They also help attract tourism, Maine's leading industry. Farms provide land critical to wildlife habitat, hunting, fishing, and snowmobiling.

The struggle exists not because farmers remain rooted in the past. Few enterprises can match the dairy farmer in efficiency. His output per worker has more than doubled during the past twenty-five years due to greater mechanization and facility advances, computer technology, improved genetics, and modern practices.

Such change is necessary because Maine producers face higher production costs than their counterparts in other states, such as New York, Pennsylvania, Wisconsin and California. One recent trend is the production of organic milk as a niche market. Roughly sixty-two of the state's dairy producers now supply the organic market, particularly smaller farms that need the higher price. A few others process milk on the farm for fluid consumption, or for value-added products such as cheese and butter.

To counter the cost–price squeeze facing the future of the dairy industry in Maine, the Governor's Task Force on the Sustainability of the Dairy Industry in Maine was formed in April

2003. The twenty-member task force featured a broad representation of individuals with an array of agricultural and economic interests. The final report, dated November 18, 2003, contains seventeen specific recommendations concerning strategies and policy making to support and enhance the dairy industry.

The recommendations include: setting price supports when the milk price falls below the short-run cost of production; property tax relief; a Dairy Management Improvement Fund; estate planning; and support for value-added processing. The report is now in the hands of Governor John Baldacci, who will work with the legislature to weigh proposals against public acceptance. Much discussion will take place before they adopt any of the recommendations.

Despite the current crisis, there is a future for the dairy industry in Maine. As former Commissioner of Agriculture Joe Williams has professed, there will always be a place for dairying and livestock in Maine, to utilize the many acres of land best suited for grass. There are opportunities for producers to become more profitable and options for adapting to new markets. And there are strategies to stabilize the price Maine farmers receive for their product.

Such efforts are important if dairy farms, like Craneland Farm, are to survive into the future and continue providing a stable economic core for rural Maine. To lose the family farm would be tragic. As Trudy captures so well in her book, such things as the joy of rural life, the pleasure of fiddlehead greens in the spring, the rolling fields, the beauty of a sunrise over the ridge and the sense of accomplishment are all precious indeed.

Chad Arms
Retired, Extension Dairy Specialist
April 2004

Author's Note

Nearly twenty years ago, a group of four women met at my farmhouse in Waldo County, Maine, to start Freedom Writers, a small writing group named after the nearby town of Freedom. Each of us already had works in progress and needed feedback. All four of us were schoolteachers — the three other women were still active while I had "retired" to work full time on my family's dairy farm. The long hours of farming chores always made finding time to write difficult — a virtual extravagance, actually. But the group's support was helpful. If the women arrived at my house while I was still out on the tractor, they would come find me and haul me off and back to the house for our meeting. At the time, I had just started to write stories about the farm, my family, the animals, and our neighbors, but I didn't know what to do with the pieces. Nor did I know if they were any good. The first time I sat before the writing group to read something I had written, I hyperventilated.

For about four years in the late 1980s, we met monthly to read our work and offer suggestions and encouragement. We rewrote, revised and read our works again and again and again. During our four years together, two members saw their books published. Sheila Gilluly published *Greenbriar Queen*, the first in a fantasy trilogy, and Katie Johnson published *Doing Words: Using the Creative Power of Children's Personal Images to Teach Reading and Writing*. In 1994, Pennelle Chase co-authored with Jane Doan, *Full Circle: A New Look at Multiage Education*. As for me, I took a little longer to get over the hump. I was technically "published" in 1988 when I began writing essays that appeared occasionally in *The* (Belfast) *Republican Journal*. This gave my confidence a big lift and started me on a roll. I began revisiting my twenty years of farm life and the stories just poured out. I sometimes wrote late into the night, sometimes all night, leaving me exhausted before I even started my morning barn chores.

And then it was all over. I gave up the farming life in 1989 and put my stories "under the bed."

During the 1990s, I went to work for Maine Writers & Publishers Alliance in Brunswick, and there I met the late John N. Cole, a wonderful Maine writer who also taught classes to help writers publish nonfiction. I decided to drag out my stories and read them again. As the cliché goes, I laughed, I cried — and I still loved them. Aided by some distance and perspective, I rewrote them. And now, finally, with *The Cows Are Out!*, I have taken the plunge of placing them before the court of public opinion.

I certainly hope readers will find some measure of humor in these pages and identify in some way with the autobiographical sketches and descriptions of a wonderful, but fading way of life in Maine — the family farm. I also hope people will gain a new appreciation of the dairy farm and farmers in general.

I know I have grown a lot since my early farming days in the 1960s. And those evenings sitting around my living room with the Freedom Writers also seem like such a long time ago. On the other hand, not everything has changed. As I present this collection to you, I am still hyperventilating.

Trudy Chambers Price
Brunswick, Maine
April 2004

Dawn:

A Prologue

I was born loving horses.

I grew up in the Aroostook County town of Caribou and every year it was a family tradition to attend the Fourth of July celebration in Houlton, about fifty miles away. My mother, Martha, packed a picnic lunch and the family — my mom, my dad, Asher, my brother, Jerome, and I — would spread out a blanket near the racetrack at the fairgrounds to eat and watch the horse races. My mom said that as soon as I could walk, I would jump up and down every time the horses rounded the track and passed us.

It was not just a summer love affair. Every Christmas I asked Santa for a horse and every year I received a doll instead. I finally accepted the fact that there was no place at our house in town to keep a horse. However, I did have friends with horses, so I took every opportunity to ride with them in the countryside where they lived. But I never gave up on my dream of owning my *own* horse and riding through my *own* fields.

Aroostook County, of course, is potato country, and was especially so in the 1940s and 1950s. As fishing was in coastal towns, so was potato farming in The County — both a job and a culture. Every aspect of our town revolved around the rhythms and cycles of the potato farmers. The school principal overlooked absent students when they were needed to help with the spring planting. One of the most active clubs in school was Future Farmers of America. Schools were closed for the four-week potato

Christening Day in Caribou, 1941. From left to right are my mother, Martha; my father, Asher; my brother, Jerome; me and Aunt Tot (Dorothy).

harvest from September 15 to October 15 so students could work in the fields. During the fall, entire families went into the fields to work and, in some cases, earn their entire annual income. Aroostook County provided a heritage of hard work.

My parents were not farmers; instead, my father was a plumber and my mother an artist. But growing up in a potato-farming community certainly influenced me and nurtured in me a true love of the outdoors. Like many other kids in The County, I began picking potatoes at the age of ten for twenty-five cents a barrel. Most every potato farmer owned an old bus and picked up whole neighborhoods of kids before dawn and then delivered them back home again in time for supper. My mother got up at four in the morning to prepare a hot breakfast for my brother and me, and to fill our black metal lunch boxes. Most mornings we wore all the clothes we could to stave off the cold, but by ten o'clock we stripped down to jeans and a T-shirt. It was common to wear out a pair of brown cotton gloves in a single day of picking potatoes. I can still smell the tops, the new potatoes, and the dirt they came from. Likewise, I can still hear the *putt, putt, putt* of the tractor and the squeaky digger approaching my section of the field.

Picking potatoes didn't pay that well, but I loved to work — and it did change my life. It was in a potato field owned by one of my parents' friends that I got to know my future husband, Ronald Price. When I was a junior at Caribou High School, Ron was the new guy in town. He had moved to The County from New Mexico, and wore moccasins, a T-shirt, Levi's, a leather jacket and a crew cut. Ron was nothing short of revolutionary, since every other teenage boy I knew wore white bucks, button-down collars, gray flannel slacks and a DA haircut. I noticed him on the very first day of school.

Every student I knew at Caribou High either picked potatoes or drove a potato truck. Ron didn't have a job, but he did

Lunch break in the Aroostook County potato fields, 1957. That's Ron, me and Al Getz.

have a license and a polished, light blue '50 Ford Crestliner. In the fall of 1957, he offered to drive me to and from the potato field if I could get him a job. I found one for him picking potatoes for fifty cents a barrel. The job just happened to be in the same field where I worked. Ron picked the section next to me and he could fill a barrel in about six to ten minutes. (Later, he told me that he hated picking potatoes, but took the job just to be near me.)

Ron and I talked while we picked and ate lunch. I learned that he had Maine roots. His parents were not farmers, but his grandparents were, and he had worked summers on their dairy farm in the Waldo County town of Knox. He decided at a very young age that his goal was to become a dairy farmer.

Future farmers. Ron and me outside my house on the day we graduated from Caribou High School, June 20, 1958.

During our senior year, Ron asked me to go steady. That year he also made me a very simple promise that touched my heart and stirred childhood dreams. "Marry me," he said, "and you can have your horse."

Ron and I graduated from Caribou High School in 1958, and then from the University of Maine in 1962, he with a degree in animal science, I with a teaching degree. We got engaged during our junior year. After graduation, we temporarily heeded a different call — one a long way from farming. We spent three years in Virginia and North Carolina while Ron served as an officer in the U.S. Marine Corps. The start of that particular three-year era was a whirlwind itself. On a single day in 1962, Ron was commissioned Second Lieutenant in the USMC, we graduated from the University of Maine, and we were married. Funny thing is, the whirlwind never really slowed down.

In 1966, we finally found ourselves back in Maine, now with two young sons, and we jumped at the chance to purchase a working dairy farm in Waldo County, high on Knox Ridge, with Mount Katahdin looming in the distance. Our new farm came complete with one hundred fifty acres, a milking herd of twenty-five registered Holsteins and their offspring — and a lot of hard work.

So, by March of 1966, I was on a farm, living the life that Ron and I had planned for nearly a decade. For the next twenty-three years, I would stay on Knox Ridge working sunup to sundown until my bones ached. Eventually, I even rode my own dream horse.

In more ways than one.

ONE

Dream Farm

Early one April morning in the mid-1980s as I left the house and started for the barn, a bitter wind blew the hood of my sweatshirt straight up and over the back of my head. I returned to the house and pulled on the wool stocking cap that I had been trying to shed for several days — not so much because I didn't need it anymore, but thinking that if I didn't wear it, the weather might just get warmer. Naive optimism, I guess.

Once inside the milk room, I drained two quarts of warm milk into two pails from the receiving jar where the milk was held before it was pumped into a one thousand-gallon cooling and storage tank. Then I stood over the deep, stainless steel sinks and added warm water to the pails so I could feed the first two of ten heifer calves at the far end of the barn ell. While working, I watched through the window as the cold, damp wind made waves on the half-frozen puddles as it whipped down our driveway. In winter, it was an unfortunate fact that if there was so much as a slight breeze elsewhere in Waldo County, it was downright windy on Knox Ridge. On the plus side, that same wind blew away blackflies and mosquitoes in the summer.

Directly across the driveway sat an old icehouse, located where Susan Crane Van Norden's mobile home once stood. That trailer had now been gone nineteen years. It didn't seem possible. My mind drifted back two decades to another cold and windy spring, and I just could not believe it had been that long since my husband Ron and I had followed our dream and come to Knox Ridge.

Time flies like the wind across our fields.

In the summer of 1964, Ron and I were in Maine on leave from the U.S. Marine Corps. Ron had begun a three-year stint in 1962. During that visit, Ron's grandfather, John W. Ingraham Sr., confided to Ron that Uncle Albert and Aunt Lona Ingraham were thinking about selling their dairy farm in Waldo County. After more than ten years of farming on his own, Albert's health problems would prevent him from milking the cows much longer.

John W. Ingraham Sr., me and Carrie Ingraham at Gold Top Farm, Knox, Maine, in January 1963. John and Carrie, Ron's grandparents, ran Gold Top Farm for 65 years.

Farming on Knox Ridge would be like coming home for Ron. During the summers of his youth, Ron had worked for Albert, another uncle, John Jr., and his grandfather, all three of whom had been in business together at Gold Top Farm.

Unfortunately, the timing wasn't right. Ron still had another year of active service. However, after much deliberation, Uncle Albert said that if he had to sell the farm, he would rather sell it to family. He said if we were serious, he and Aunt Lona would work the farm for another year until Ron was discharged.

During our college days, we had regularly visited Knox Ridge. But on that summer day I went to Uncle Albert's barn with a new perspective. Maybe, I thought, this farm and these cows will be ours in a year. I watched Uncle Albert, then in his late forties, dressed in his coveralls, graining the cows before he began the afternoon milking. I watched Aunt Lona in her kerchief and boots using a hoe to scrape back the manure from under the cows and into the gutter behind them as she prepared to run the gutter cleaner — a 140-foot chain in the gutter that carried the manure out to the manure shed and into the spreader. I imagined myself in her boots. I breathed in the barn smells — the cows' spicy breath, the sweet smell of hay, and the strong scent of urine and manure. Guess I can handle this, I thought, so long as I can have my horse.

The next day, I continued north to Caribou. Kyle, our fifteen-month-old son, and I spent the summer with my family there while Ron cruised the Caribbean aboard the aircraft carrier USS *Boxer*. With the Knox Ridge farm seemingly in our future, we finally had an answer when people asked us what we planned to do after the Corps: We would buy the family farm and milk cows.

After Ron's discharge from the Marines a year later in 1965, we stayed with his parents in Brewer while we made the necessary

Photo courtesy of Jolene Littlefield

A late 1800s photograph of the Vose farm on Knox Ridge, a place that would eventually become our dream farm.

arrangements to buy the farm. After we agreed upon a price, we applied to the Farmers Home Administration (FHA) for financing. A month later, the FHA supervisor called us in for a meeting.

We were shocked to learn from Mr. Osgood that the county FHA committee hadn't approved our loan application. Ron and I looked at each other in disbelief.

"But why not?" Ron asked. "We certainly must be qualified. We both have college degrees and mine is in Animal Science. I have work experience on a dairy farm — not milking cows, but I'm sure I can learn that quickly. What's the reason?"

"I don't think you'd be satisfied with the income that twenty-five cows provide, and the farm doesn't have enough land base to expand the herd," Mr. Osgood told us. "Albert rents forty acres from his cousin next door. What happens if Dick wants to use his land for himself? There wouldn't be enough land to feed even twenty-five cows."

"We don't plan to expand," Ron said. "Twenty-five cows are enough and I've already spoken to Dick and he says we can have the same arrangement as he had with Uncle Albert, at least

4

for a while. Even if we decide to expand later, there must be land available to rent on The Ridge."

"Not much," Mr. Osgood explained. "There are dairy farms all around Albert's farm, ten just in Knox alone. The competition for land is quite strong. And what would you do if ten cows got sick and died the first year?"

"I don't know," Ron said despondently. "I really don't know. I guess I'd take things as they come."

Mr. Osgood leaned forward over his desk and looked directly at me, then at Ron. "You both have a college education and could get good-paying jobs. You don't want to go down on the farm and eat peanut butter and jelly sandwiches the rest of your lives."

I felt tears building. Who is this man to deny us our dream? Who does he think he is?

Little did I know then that he was right — that there wasn't enough land, and we would have to milk more cows to pay the debts. He was challenging us, trying to find out just how much we wanted to farm. He was doing his job. He was testing us — and all I could do was shake my head and cry.

"I like peanut butter and jelly sandwiches," Ron said after we returned to the car. "Who does he think he is, trying to tell us what we want and don't want? We'll find another farm and apply again."

When we reported the news that our FHA loan had been denied, Uncle Albert said he would have to look for another buyer.

The only other farm for sale in the area was a well-kept, but very old farm in Appleton. It would have cost too much to modernize. With no good farm prospect in sight, our search cooled. At the time, we were living with my in-laws, with our two small sons, Kyle, two years old, and Travis, five months old.

It was growing tiresome and we were anxious to settle else-where. I'm sure my in-laws felt the same way.

At the University of Maine placement center, Ron found an opening for an assistant foreman on an apple, beef and turkey farm in Millis, Massachusetts. Intrigued, we both went for the interview in Boston, where we met Mr. Paine of the stock bro-kerage firm Paine, Webber, Jackson and Curtis. After a brief interview, the farm foreman took us on a tour of the four-hun-dred-acre farm, twenty-five miles southeast of Boston. Ron accepted the job, and two weeks later, we moved into a newly renovated house on the farm.

Ron soon discovered that improving efficiency and imple-menting new technology were not part of the overall farm plan. Once when he suggested an easier way to feed silage to the cat-tle, the hired men just looked at him and said, "We've always done it this way." Most of his suggestions met the same fate.

By Christmas, Ron knew that Mr. Paine didn't need or want efficiency, change or progress on the farm. He also didn't need premium prices for his apples. It didn't matter whether Ron did well at his job or not — the farm would endure.

From then on, the relationship between the hired men and Ron was cool at best. They ignored him most of the time and the foreman treated him like the others.

Because we lived in Massachusetts, Ron had the option of continuing his military service as a reserve officer. He spent one weekend a month at South Weymouth Naval Air Station. One Sunday night he returned with a satisfied smirk on his face.

"Guess what?" he quizzed me, not waiting for me to answer. "All I have to do is sign on the dotted line and my orders will be cut for flight training in Pensacola, Florida."

"What are you talking about?" I dropped my book in my lap.

"I took the written flight test and aced it. All I have to do is sign. It would solve the job situation."

I gulped. "You know what happens to pilots who graduate from flight school? They go straight to Vietnam. That's where your friends who stayed in the Corps are right now."

I remembered how much he had wanted to be a pilot when he was on active duty, but hadn't passed the test.

"What do you say?" he went on.

"I say, fine, go ahead if you want to, but I'm going home to Maine — I don't want to be a widow!"

He abandoned the idea. But he remained desperate to get off the Massachusetts farm.

That February, a letter arrived from Aunt Lona. She and Uncle Albert had sold the farm to a young woman, Susan Crane Van Norden of New York. She was living with them to learn the dairy farming business. The papers would be signed and passed in March and she would need a farm manager. She had advertised for an older couple, got no responses, and then advertised again for a couple with no children, with still no responses. Aunt Lona had suggested Ron and told us to call if we were interested.

Ron quickly set up an interview. When he got off the phone, Ron did a little dance around the kitchen. "Now all I have to do is sell myself. Dream Farm, here we come."

After agreeing on the job and salary, Susan hired Ron as farm manager of the newly named Craneland Farm. She said that she expected him to run the farm as if it were his own. He told her how important it was to him that the farm be self-sufficient because he was leaving a job where that wasn't the case. Susan assured him that was her goal.

Ron returned to Massachusetts and gave his two-weeks' notice. Meanwhile, Uncle Albert, Aunt Lona and Susan moved

Ron, Kyle, Travis and me in Brewer, Maine, June 1965.

out of the main house so we could live there, and took an apart-
ment in the neighboring town of Brooks.

We arrived back in Maine for good in the middle of the night
on Kyle's third birthday, March 17, 1966. Behind our 1962 Ford
was the biggest U-Haul trailer made. Even in the late-winter darkness, we could see the big, two-story white farmhouse, the long,
red shed that stretched toward the 101-foot barn that snugly and
silently housed the twenty-five cows and their babies of all ages —
cows and babies that we would milk and care for. Uncle Albert
had put down planks in the muddy driveway to let us know where
to drive our heavy rig. We were tired, but excited.

Kyle and Travis were asleep on the backseat. Neither of
them would remember any other life but growing up on the farm.

During that first nasty April, Susan and Uncle Albert came
to the farm every day. They taught Ron how to milk cows. They

helped with the chores and they set up a home for Susan, a large, comfortable mobile home across the driveway from the farmhouse.

During the next few months, we entered the busiest time of the year on the farm — spring and summer. We worked long and hard and learned the farm life — everything from milking, feeding, and breeding the cows to caring for calves, baling hay, and planting the garden. I met the rest of Ron's family, got to know the neighbors, and made new friends. We were quickly absorbed into the community and loved the rural life of which we had dreamed.

Then, only eight months later, Susan married a local farmer and decided to sell Craneland Farm. To show how much she appreciated our work, she gave us the first option to buy. If we could get an FHA loan for the real estate, she would personally finance the cattle and machinery. Her only request was that we keep the name Craneland Farm. "If it hadn't been for my Uncle Clinton Crane," Susan said, "neither one of us would have had a chance at farming this place."

This time, we had all the answers for the FHA and we were in a much better position. Susan had purchased both a new tractor and a new truck and had installed a pipeline in the barn that eliminated the need to lift ten-gallon milk cans. Now the milk went directly from the cow through a pipeline into the milk room, and then into the bulk tank.

Our Dream Farm became a reality on November 7, 1966.

From that day on we looked at the farm differently. The eleven-room house with twenty-two windows was pretty much mine. I could paint or decorate any way that I chose, and Susan generously let us keep most of the furnishings.

Ron's interests lay out the back door. As Uncle Albert used to say, "No trouble getting to work in the morning. Just go out

Our Dream Farm. An aerial photograph of Craneland Farm at about the time we bought it in the mid-1960s.

the back door, through the connected sixty-foot shed, and there's the barn door, ten feet away." Behind the shed stood a thirty-foot chicken house where I would eventually keep laying hens and raise pigs. The forty-acre field rose from the farm to a rock wall bordering our neighbors' farm, owned by Dick and Amy Ingraham. Dick was Ron's cousin. The other one hundred acres gradually sloped to woods, where heifers roamed in the summer and where prime lumber stood waiting.

Along with owning a farm came the reality of endless hard work, responsibility and bills. But also, there was the belief that we could build equity for the future, know the security of living in a rural town where crime was practically nonexistent, and raise our sons in beautiful surroundings.

Our roots would grow deep during the next twenty years.
They grew through many a beautiful summer day and long
winter night, and even through many cold April days like this
one that no amount of optimism could truly warm.

THE COWS ARE OUT!

Two

Long Days on the Farm

An early spring our first year gave us time to settle into the big farmhouse and watch our fields turn green, while at the same time learning the daily routine of milking and feeding the cows, feeding the calves, and cleaning the barn. Uncle Albert and Aunt Lona told us what they had done in previous springs: fences were repaired so that cows and young stock could go outside for the summer; tractors, trucks and other equipment were readied for summer use; the barn was cleaned for a new crop of hay; the garden was planted.

With summer came haying season — mowing the fields, conditioning the hay by running it through rollers to squeeze out the moisture, raking the cut hay and then baling it before loading it onto trailers and taking it to the barn for storage. After the first crop of hay was in, a second crop was ready. Of course, the garden had to be weeded and harvested, too.

During the fall, manure was spread on the fields, wood was put in to heat the house, garden vegetables were preserved and buildings repaired, painted and buttoned up for winter. There was also plenty to do in the winter. Because the livestock were

The first load of hay coming in behind a Farmall 200 tractor, June 1966. Ron is driving. The crew includes Jackie Parker, a friend from North Carolina who came to see if we were really farming!

confined, there was more work inside the barn: manure to clean out, cows to clip and brush so they stayed clean and cool, and more time feeding the animals — not to mention everything necessary to keep the barn and milk room from freezing up. The yard and barnyard had to be kept clear of snow so the milk truck could pick up milk every other day and so the cows could get outside for exercise. And, as during every season, the cows had to be milked twice daily. Cows don't take days off, not even Christmas.

Every eight weeks, no matter the season, we stopped everything except barn chores to clean out several of our neighbors' chicken houses after their broilers had been picked up for slaughter in Belfast. A bucket tractor was used to load the chicken manure into a spreader for spreading on our fields, or to pile it for future use. It made excellent fertilizer.

We were learning the business of dairy farming. Our primary income was from the sale of milk to Oakhurst Dairy in Portland. They picked up our milk every other day and trucked it to Portland for processing. Our milk tank held 500 gallons at the time (we later upgraded to a 1,000-gallon tank). However, we were not paid by the gallon, but rather by hundredweight of milk shipped. We were paid twice each month. The advance check we received was half of the estimated production for the month. The final check arrived minus our FHA mortgage

Ron and me planting the garden.

Travis (on the left) and Kyle with Alex in 1968.

payment, which Oakhurst withheld and sent directly to FHA. Our other income came from the sale of unproductive cows — cows whose age or health may have prevented pregnancy — for beef and bull calves for veal. Occasionally, a good cow was sold as breeding stock. The bills had to be paid from those income sources — and the bills seemed overwhelming. I kept our unpaid bills not in a shoebox, but a boot box. And that boot box bulged. The mortgage payment to Susan was at the top of the list. Next came payments for loans on the mower and baler, bills for grain, cow bedding, fuel, electricity, fertilizer, veterinary care and medicine, breeding, labor, registration of purebred heifer calves, barn and milk room supplies, machinery repairs and upkeep of the property. During the first two to three years, we actually were able to keep up with the bills, but as improvements, renovations and new machinery were needed, the accumulating debt put us further and further behind.

During those early days, we became acclimated to our daily chores, but there was something about Sunday mornings that was different. I hated to get up. Maybe it was because I longed for one day — or even just one morning — off. I would roll over and lie an extra ten minutes in the warm bed, simply delaying the inevitable.

Ron was usually gone from our bed an hour and a half before the alarm went off for me at five o'clock. I wondered how he stood it day in and day out.

Later, when I asked him about those mornings, he said the first year was the hardest. After just seven months of getting up every morning at half past three, he asked himself, "Why?"

"It has to be a love affair with cows," I responded. "I could never do what you do. If something happened to you, I'd sell the farm."

But he did do it. In fact, he thrived on it. After he became accustomed to rising early, he cherished the quiet time to meditate, plan his day's activities, sort out priorities, and solve the world's problems. Each morning as Ron flipped on the barn lights, the cows rose in their stalls and watched as he pushed the grain cart to apportion their feed. They responded to his good husbandry by giving all the milk they could.

Typical Day at Craneland Farm

3:30 A.M.
> Milker rises to grain and milk cows

5:30 A.M.
> Feed calves milk and grain, bed down
> Wash milk dishes
> Let cows outside for exercise while milking barn is cleaned —
> run gutter cleaner, scrape stalls, bed down with fresh sawdust
> Apportion grain and forage
> Clean the out (secondary) barns
> Feed dry cows and mature heifers
> Let cows in and tie up (cows stay outside at night during the
> summer)

9:00 A.M.
> Breakfast break

10:00 A.M.
> Summer (in between chores): mow, ted, rake hay for either
> baling or chopping
> Store baled hay in barn or haylage in silo
> Repair and maintain machinery
> Perform veterinary care, give medications or treatments
> Breed cows
> Haul sawdust
> Eat lunch
> Attend agricultural meetings
> Do bookkeeping
> Be a plumber, electrician, carpenter, or mechanic as needed
> Do gardening, house chores and cooking, mow lawn
> Spread manure (seasonal)

3:30 P.M.
> Repeat morning chores (cows stay inside at night in winter)

6:00 P.M.
> Supper
> Read agricultural publications
> Watch a little television
> Collapse into bed

Note: At any time of day or night, during any season, help deliver
calves and attend to sick animals

THREE

Paying the Bills: A Reluctant Teacher

One morning at breakfast about three years after we had bought Craneland Farm, Ron announced that he thought we should buy a mowing machine so that we would not need to depend on Dick, who had to do his own haying and keep up with his corn-spraying business. I understood Ron's reasoning. Our only crop was hay. When conditions are ideal, you need to get out and mow the hay the minute it is ready. A delay means the hay may get too mature and lose nutritional value. If you own your machine, then you can take responsibility for the upkeep and fix it quickly if it breaks down, not wait for your cousin to do so. In addition, a new mower should not break down as often, allowing us to mow faster.

His reasons were all sound, but, as usual, my Aroostook County upbringing came into play. I was taught that you earn the money first, and then you buy what you want or need. That old Maine Yankee ethic was deeply ingrained in my psyche. Given our existing farm debt, I was hesitant to take on any more payments.

The Chambers clan at Craneland Farm, October 1968. Standing from left is Asher (my father), Ron, Travis, Betheny (my sister), Jerome (my brother) and his wife Ella, Karen Lipka and Gwenn Lipka (two of Ella's daughters), and me. Sitting from left is Kyle, Martha (my mother), Cindy Lipka and Martha Jean Chambers (my niece).

"We can't afford a new mowing machine," I said. "And it doesn't just end with a mowing machine — we would also need a hay conditioner, a rake, a baler and trailers."

I knew all that would cost thousands of dollars that we didn't have.

"I think Dick would let us use his conditioner and rake and I could build some hay trailers," Ron argued, "but we *would* need a baler. Maybe we could find a secondhand mower and baler. I have until next spring to look around for them."

Ron didn't waste any time and by early winter he had found a mower and baler even though there was no money to buy them. We were keeping up with our mortgage payments and bills but we couldn't take on any more debt.

Then he dropped the big one.

After we had eaten lunch and the boys were napping, Ron set aside his pulverized toothpick and cleared his throat.

"What would you think about getting a job?" Ron asked.

"A job? I have a job," I said. "Right here — helping with the chores, taking care of the house, cooking and looking after the boys."

"I mean a job off the farm," he said, "like teaching school to bring in the extra money we need to buy the mower and baler."

"I don't know," I said. "We would have to hire a babysitter for the boys."

"I could take care of them," Ron said, "take them along when I go for a load of sawdust. They like to ride in the truck. And they could go to the barn with me at chore time."

"They're only three and five," I argued. "They still need naps. And what if one gets sick?"

"I can put them down for naps," Ron said. "I don't mind — although there might be some days when we would need a sitter if I have to work outside."

"Let me sleep on the idea," I said.

I had received a five-year Maine teacher's certificate after I graduated from the University of Maine in 1962. And I had taught in Virginia for three months, but had not been in a classroom since that time. By this time, my teaching certificate had expired; I would have to work as a substitute and then get a temporary certificate if the school really wanted me. Teachers were scarce in the late 1960s, so it would probably not be much of a problem.

The next morning at breakfast, Ron was back on the subject.

"Well, have you thought it over — about getting a job?" he asked. He tilted his chair back and ran his hand over the top of his still-short, military-style haircut.

"I'd rather not leave the boys to go to work," I said, "but I don't see any other way to buy the equipment we need."

I actually hated the idea. I got up from my chair, cleared the dishes and went to the kitchen.

Even though the 1968–1969 school year was half over, Ron urged me to inquire about a teaching job immediately. The boys listened intently to our conversation.

"Where are you going, Mommy?" asked five-year-old Kyle.

"Nowhere yet, but I might get a job," I replied.

"Who will take care of Travis and me?"

"Probably Daddy. Would you like to help Daddy with the farm chores if I got a job teaching school?"

"Yeah," Kyle answered with a smile. Travis just shook his head sideways.

I met with the local superintendent and he said a third-grade teacher was set to leave after Christmas to have a baby. The job was mine if I wanted it. I accepted. Maybe I could earn enough money to buy my horse, too, I thought.

After the holidays, despite my doubts, I began teaching thirty-two third-graders. I would make less than $7,000 a year.

At the end of each day, as soon as the boys saw my car come into the yard, they ran from the barn to the house.

"What did you do today, boys?" I asked one day, as I helped Travis unzip his jacket.

"We helped Dad unload a load of sawdust upstairs in the barn," Kyle said. "Travis and I shoveled and shoveled. Then we had to call the vet because Mazie had twins and one came backwards."

the milk tank before he did afternoon chores. That would give him time to start the fencing. I would miss taking part in the fence work this year. I really enjoyed that chore — the trek around the fence line, over the rocky pasture, through the woods along the property line, eating picnic lunches near the brook. I would also miss the anticipation of budding leaves and a green tinge on the pasture. I would miss coming across the old sap camp and hearing the story again of how years ago, the trees used to be tapped and maple syrup boiled right there in our woods. I would miss turning out the bred heifers from their winter confinement into summer freedom. I felt I was living on my dream farm, but missing out on all the benefits.

That afternoon as I stood on my tiptoes and scrubbed the inside of the five hundred-gallon milk tank with a long-handled brush, I wondered why I enjoyed this chore so much today. Was it because it was Friday and there was no school the next day? I'd be home tomorrow to eat lunch with my family and play a game with the boys after they napped.

Three weeks before the end of the school year, I told Ron that I had been offered a job for the fall and I had to let them know by the first of August.

"I think you should tell them right now that you'll be back in the fall," Ron said. "We haven't paid off the mower and baler yet."

No, we hadn't. The money I earned teaching was not much, and what there was kept getting diverted. I also didn't have a horse yet, I thought, which had been part of the deal. Because of these issues, I accepted the job.

That summer, I dove into farm work with new perspective. I relished the hours raking hay in the open fields, not confined by a classroom. I enjoyed my boys, just the two of them. When I flopped into bed at night, it was a satisfying *physical* tired, not mental exhaustion. The back of my neck hadn't ached since school ended. I'll be more organized when I return to school in the fall, I thought. I'll freeze some meals that I can fix quickly when I get home. I'll do a little housework each day and then it won't get ahead of me. I'll do my lesson plans this summer and maybe next year's class will be smaller and easier. Maybe, it will all work out. Maybe.

That fall, I had my photograph taken at school with the children. I showed it to my mother when we made our annual trip to Caribou after Christmas.

"This is my class, Ma; aren't they cute?"

"Yes, they're cute, but you look tired."

"I do?" I examined my photo more closely.

"One eye is drooping and your smile is strained," she pointed out, "and look at the dark circles under your eyes."

I went to look in the mirror. She was right.

"I'm leading four lives," I told her. "Mother, housewife, teacher and farmer. Anyone would be tired."

"I think you're doing too much," she said. "Why don't you give up the teaching so you can be home with the boys?" That was her mantra.

My mother had been a stay-at-home mom and firmly believed that's what mothers should do. Just as traditionally, my father was proud to be the breadwinner so that she could do that. Neither she nor my father was pleased when Ron and I decided that we wanted to have a dairy farm, because they knew it meant hard work for both of us. Ron's parents, Clarence and Alcadia, weren't happy with our decision, either. Both of them grew up on dairy farms and vowed to have nothing to do with them as adults. Alcadia had sworn from an early age that she would never

Dad helping me bring in some vegetables at Craneland Farm. Dad worried that farming was going to make me old before I turned fifty.

marry a farmer. Clarence and Alcadia, who worried about the financial drain, even went to my parents with their concerns about our decision, a meeting we never heard about until years later. My parents told them they had concerns, too, but that they would not discourage us if that was what we really wanted.

And now, after just a short time on the farm, my mother's concerns were becoming a reality. It was hard work. I was tired. Both she and my father were afraid for my health. Whenever my parents visited us, my father always helped with the chores.

After he died, my mother told me that he didn't enjoy the work, but he did it to help me. He was afraid I'd be an old woman before I turned fifty.

Despite all this, I taught third grade for another year and helped at the farm on weekends and whenever I could fit it into my schedule. I did not, however, work before leaving for school each morning.

As that school year drew to a close in the spring of 1970, even though the baler and mower loan (our first "operating loan") were still not paid off, I told Ron that I didn't want to teach another year. I wanted to be home with him and the boys. One of the reasons we decided to farm was so that we could be together. I felt in limbo, just existing instead of living, as I waited for something to end.

Ron had hoped that I would continue teaching, but he understood why I wanted to be home. It hadn't been easy for him, either. He admitted that he had been impatient with the boys and frustrated when he needed help with a project in my absence. He said that things went better when I was home.

Of course, there was still the issue of how we were going to pay all the bills. Ron simply offered the solution that all dairy farmers give when faced with mounting debt.

"We'll just milk a few more cows."

FOUR

Jud

There was one thing during the days when I tried to balance both teaching and working on the farm that helped me alleviate stress and occasionally convince me that all was right with the world: his name was Jud.

One morning before I left for school, Ron asked me to make a couple of extra sandwiches for Bill Morse who was coming to trim the cows' overgrown hooves.

Bill was an important part of maintaining our herd's health. Overgrown hooves can cause lameness, unnatural gait and other problems. Most critically, especially for a dairy farm, cows with healthy feet produce more milk.

At supper that night Bill invited us to take a trip to New York and Vermont with him and his wife. He had seen the daughters of some bulls he thought could help us improve our herd genetics. He wanted to show us the farms and the cows.

"If I'm going to take time off, I'm not sure I want to look at cows," I said. "I can see cows at home."

Bill assured me it would be a one-day trip.

"How about next Saturday? You be at our house in Oxford

by five o'clock in the morning and we'll be back home by midnight."

"Why don't you go, Ron," I suggested. "I think I'd rather stay home."

"Would you go if we looked at a horse, too?" Ron asked.

I glanced at Bill. He looked guilty. I realized the two men had planned the whole thing.

"I'll probably be in trouble for the rest of my life for telling you where that horse is," Bill said. "I know your husband isn't fond of horses — they don't give milk and they do eat hay — but I have to do something to get you away from here to see how other farmers operate."

Here's my chance to get a horse, I thought; but all the way to Vermont? I could look for a horse around here . . . but the time was right and I trusted Bill's judgment. If he knows a beautiful cow when he sees one, why not a beautiful horse?

"I'll forgive you, Bill," Ron said. "Besides, I have to live up to my word. I promised Trudy she could have a horse if she married me."

Yes, he certainly did. I decided to go.

Ron and I met Bill and Beulah in Oxford early that Saturday morning. We visited five dairy farms in New York and saw hundreds of cows. On the way home we stopped at a farm in Richmond, Vermont. I don't remember any of the cows I saw during the twenty-three-hour trip, but it was love at first sight when I saw Jud. Jud belonged to the farmer's daughter, but she had grown up and gone away to college. They wanted to sell him — but not to just anybody. They wanted him to go to a farm where he'd get good care.

Jud was born right there on the farm. The Verchereau family had boarded a famous Morgan stallion for their vet one winter,

Jud at Craneland Farm, January 1970.

and for payment, he had bred their pinto mare to his stallion. Jud had his mother's red and white markings, but the thick neck and height of his Morgan sire. He was shaggy because he still had his winter coat, but the owner assured me that when he shed out, he was sleek and shiny. I believed her.

"He's beautiful," I exclaimed.

Jud hadn't been ridden for two years and I wondered if I could ride a horse that hadn't been ridden for so long. I wrote a check for $250 — the best $250 I ever spent. It probably should have gone toward the mower, but for once, farm equipment took the backseat.

31

When we got home I went to see my friend, neighbor and farrier, Roy Bessey, and asked him what he thought of buying a horse that hadn't been ridden for two years.

"I'd be more concerned about a horse having good feet," Roy replied. "A horse that has been well trained never forgets it, but if he doesn't have sound feet, what good is the rest of him?"

I admitted that I hadn't examined his feet closely, but had noticed they were white and looked long and ragged.

"White feet are usually soft," Roy said. "They should be trimmed when you get him home. You may have to keep shoes on him most of the time, depending on where you ride him."

"Which brings me to my next question," I said. "After I bring him home, will you ride him first? I'm nervous about that and I've had very little riding experience compared to you."

"Let's just get Jud home first," Roy said.

On Easter Sunday, we rented a horse trailer and I asked Sandy, my neighbor and babysitter, who had just lost her horse to a broken leg, to go with us to help. She brought her halter and horse blanket, so Jud wouldn't be cold on the ride home. The five of us crowded into the truck cab for the six-hour trip to Vermont.

Jud didn't like anything about his trip to Maine. He didn't know any of us, so he shied and strongly objected to our halter and rope. He had never seen a horse blanket, so he spooked when Sandy tried to throw it over him. He had never traveled, and balked at being loaded into the trailer. By then, I was having my doubts about him. To top it off, he had never been separated from his twenty-year-old pony companion and every time we led him to the trailer, he tried to return to the pasture. With Sandy's patience, we finally loaded Jud and brought him home.

I was brushing away big clumps of Jud's winter coat when Roy arrived to inspect the new horse. He advised me to attach a very long strap to Jud's halter and coax him to circle me and to conduct this "lead and lunge" exercise every day for a couple of weeks.

Two weeks later, I borrowed Sandy's saddle and Roy came for the trial ride. Roy brought along a restraining strap that hooked from Jud's bridle to a strap around his brisket so that Jud couldn't rear up. After we lunged Jud around the dooryard to get out some of the kinks, Roy helped with the bridling and saddling.

"There you go, Trudy," Roy said. "I think Jud's all ready."

I looked at him in horror. What did he mean, There you go?

"Aren't you going to ride him first?" I asked.

"He's your horse," Roy said in his soft voice, "and if you don't ride him first, he'll never really be yours."

My hands were shaking as I took the reins and the saddle horn in my left hand.and grabbed the back of the saddle with my right hand. Roy held the reins close at Jud's head while I put my foot in the stirrup. Jud pranced and sidestepped, but Roy restrained him as I swung myself up and into the saddle. Feeling Jud's uneasiness increased my own, but Roy calmed Jud as he led him around the dooryard, showing me how to hold the reins, how to set my feet in the stirrups, how to turn him, how to stop him.

Every day I rushed home from school, bridled Jud and took a short ride bareback around the farm. I saw spring come. I saw spring go. I even rode Jud in the rain. With each ride, Jud and I slowly gained confidence and trust in each other. During those rides, I could temporarily let go of all my worries about school, the farm and our bills. Even mundane home tasks seemed easier after a horseback ride.

I took every opportunity to ride Jud bareback. With my fists full of his coarse, white mane to help stay atop his smooth, warm

Me and Jud, October 1970.

back, we cantered to a rhythm known only to us. My slightest
knee pressure turned him right or left. My bare heels quickened
his pace around the edge of the field above the farm, through the
gap in the stonewall into our neighbor's fields and back again. It
was a childhood dream come true, and those rides on Jud through
my very own fields rank among the best times of my life.

FIVE

Jill

After about a year on the farm, Ron and I began to feel confident dealing with the day-to-day routine. And as time rolled along, we began to think that we were smarter than the bovines, which, after all, appear to be just big, dumb and clumsy. One day, we discovered just how clever some cows can be, and how much we still had to learn.

Jill was our biggest cow, and although we didn't know much about body conformation at the time, we thought she was beautiful. Her black, silky hide was accentuated by her straight, level back, and her shoulders blended smoothly into a wide, powerful front end. Her rump was broad and flat and her wide muzzle and deep body enabled her to eat a tremendous amount of food. Her udder shape was desirable — it was snugly attached in both front and rear, with teats plumb. She had large, bright brown eyes, and she was alert to the activities around her. Kittens playing in the hay or the rattle of the grain scoop brought Jill to her feet.

"How much do you think she weighs?" I asked Ron as we stood admiring her.

"Let's tape her and find out," he said.

Ron went to the barn medicine cabinet, pulled out the girth tape, unfolded it, and placed it over Jill's shoulders. A girth tape resembles a cloth tape measure, much like one used for sewing, but with inches on one side and pounds on the other. Inches can be converted to pounds based on averages of cattle weights. Ron reached under Jill's belly, grasped the tape, joined the ends at her side, and then slid it back and forth to a position just behind her front legs. He studied the numbers where the tape came snugly together.

"It reads ninety-three and one-half inches," Ron said, and then turned the tape over. "Eighteen hundred and fifty pounds. That's quite a cow!"

She was quite a cow at that. I clearly remember the involved process of getting her pregnant. Monitoring and impregnating a cow and then birthing the calf are not left to chance or the course of nature because it is perhaps the most critical aspect of running a successful dairy farm. It is particularly important to breed your best-producing cows because they are more likely to give birth to good-producing offspring. Still, it is quite a process that can require careful planning, time and patience.

Heifers and cows exhibit signs of estrus that must be observed and recorded, especially when artificial insemination is planned.

"Standing heat" is one of Mother Nature's indications that a female bovine is at the right stage of her estrus to conceive. Heifers begin to show signs of estrus around six months of age, and will ride piggyback on others. If the heifer being ridden stands still for the activity, she is in standing heat. While she may not be old enough to breed at that time, her name is written on the heat expectancy chart stapled to the barn wall. We used a twenty-one-day column chart to follow "heat lines" on all heifers and cows. If the animal had a regular cycle, her name would appear in a line across the chart and we would know when to expect her in heat again. She would be bred then, if she was old enough (fifteen months), or weighed enough (eight hundred pounds). Jill's line on the breeding chart showed that she had passed blood on her last cycle, which indicated that everything seemed to be functioning properly and she was ready to breed.

Ron made the usual phone call to Leander, the insemination technician for Eastern Artificial Insemination Cooperative, who was also known as "The Artificial Man." Along with traveling from farm to farm breeding cows, he offered his encouragement and philosophies to anyone who would listen.

Ron and I really needed Leander's support during our first few years of farming. We had good luck breeding the cows during the summer and fall when the cows were out to pasture and we could easily observe standing heats. But once cold weather and snow arrived, the cows were confined to the barn and standing heat was difficult to ascertain. We were inexperienced in other forms of heat detection, so many went undetected by us.

To be profitable, a dairy cow should bear a calf a year. Once she has given birth at around two years of age and her milking process has begun, breeding can start again within sixty to ninety days. The peak of her milk production will occur during the first three to four months following calving. Then it's desirable that she be bred. When a cow remains not pregnant, or "open," beyond one hundred days, despite impregnation efforts, you get concerned. Delayed conception meant a longer dry period, during which time the cow continued to eat and take up space, but wasn't productive. That was a losing equation for a dairy farm.

After Leander arrived to impregnate Jill, I went to the barn to observe, help if I could, and hear his comments.

"Hi, Ma. How's Ma today?" Leander brightened your day, no matter what. "Where's Pa today? Left you with all the work again, eh?" He squeezed my arm and smiled.

"Let's see about your cow." He pulled the long plastic glove onto his left arm and secured it to the shoulder of his coveralls by pinching the glove to the material with forceps. "I'll check her first to see how she feels."

Leander ran his glove-covered arm into Jill's rectum, removed excess manure with an in-and-out motion and, at the same time, stroked the top of her vagina through the intestinal wall. A stream of clear mucus ran from her vulva to the gutter behind her. "Running right out of her," Leander said with a wide smile, "and look at the way she's tossing her head at me. She's ready to breed. Which bull do you want to use on her?"

"We chose UNH President King," I told him. "He's supposed to increase milk production. Jill's beautiful, but she needs to put more milk in the tank."

Ron had studied the bull proofs and tried to choose specific bulls with strengths that would improve upon the weak traits of each specific cow. In Jill's case, she needed improved milk production and with luck, the genetic influence of the bull would create for her a daughter that produced more milk.

Leander returned to the milk room to prepare for the insemination. The trunk of his car held the tank of liquid nitrogen where the bull semen was stored at four hundred degrees below zero. He withdrew an ampule of King semen from the tank with tweezers and thawed it in a Thermos of water and ice cubes. He broke the nub of glass off the end of the ampule and drew the semen into a long pipette by means of a bulb similar to an eyedropper. Then he inserted a plunger into the pipette.

I stepped into the stall beside Jill and held her tail out of the way. Once again, Leander plunged his glove-covered arm into Jill's rectum and grasped her cervix through the intestinal wall. With his other hand, he inserted the breeding pipette into her vagina. By feeling the tip of her cervix with his left hand, he guided the end of the pipette through the cervix with his right hand and propelled the semen into the uterus by pushing the plunger.

"Pregnant!" Leander announced.

"I hope so," I responded.

Cows can be checked for pregnancy after thirty-five days. Since Jill did not come back into heat, we were hopeful. On his next visit, Dr. Brad Brown, our vet, confirmed her as pregnant. Success.

By the time Jill was within two weeks of giving birth, she was heavy with calf and starting to "bag" or swell. Ron was concerned that her udder was so full and tight.

Jill had spent six weeks of her two-month dry period in the dry-cow pasture where she received no grain. Pregnant bovines usually need only hay and/or forage during their dry period. Grain would cause excess body weight and is reintroduced slowly, starting a few weeks before calving. Increased amounts of grain are given as milk production increases, and cut back as milk production decreases at the end of a ten-month lactation.

Two weeks before her due date, Jill learned where her new milking stall was by going in and out of the barn with the milk cows morning and night. She was fed a small amount of grain, which was increased gradually in preparation for her calving and subsequent lactation.

Jill's udder continued to grow larger. Several days before her due date, Ron felt her udder carefully, and then looked at me with concern.

"I've never done it before," he said, "but I may have to milk this cow before she calves so the swelling doesn't injure her udder."

Jill's due date came and went and she still showed no signs of delivery. Ron milked her to relieve the pressure.

"She looks so much more comfortable," he said. "I'm sure I've made the right decision."

Ron continued to milk Jill every morning and afternoon during the end of her pregnancy. We watched her carefully for signs of impending delivery. Dr. Brown was doing a routine herd-health check one day and Ron mentioned that Jill had gone by her due date by quite a few days.

"Will you examine her to be sure everything is all right?" he asked. "I've been milking her for a week with no sign of a calf, and the last couple of days she doesn't seem to have as much milk as usual."

"Sure," Brad said. He pulled a long plastic sleeve onto his left arm and inserted it into Jill's rectum. He palpated her uterus through the rectum wall to confirm the presence of a calf. As he did so, he stretched up on his tiptoes, looked out the barn window toward the back pasture, leaned forward, and squinted for several moments. He withdrew his arm, stepped back, and studied Jill.

"This cow's not pregnant," he exclaimed.

"What?" Ron responded with alarm. "Of course she's pregnant; she's been making milk for a week."

Brad motioned for us to come to the barn window. "What's that I see down the lane there?" he asked.

We rushed to the window to see a black, shiny calf bouncing up and down, about two hundred feet away, coming toward the barn, and then turning to trot back to the pasture.

"You mean Jill's not pregnant because she's already had her calf?" Ron looked at Brad in disbelief.

"That's exactly what I mean." Brad threw his head back and laughed.

"Guess the joke's on us, isn't it?" Ron said.

"She never showed any sign of delivery, no blood, no afterbirth," I said.

"I never suspected she had already calved," Ron said. "I've had cows deliver in the pasture before and stay with their calves, so when a cow didn't appear at milking time, I went looking for her. Usually in the woods or in the farthest corner of the pasture I'd find her trying to hide her baby."

"But Jill left her calf and came to the barn just the same," I said.

"Jill's a clever cow," Brad said. "She hid her calf, all right — so well that you didn't even know she'd delivered. Coming in to be milked without the calf was her best disguise. But how do you suppose she kept the calf from following her back to the barn?"

"By feeding it before she came in; that's why she doesn't have as much milk for me," Ron said.

Outsmarted by a cow. We were humbled.

Separating the mother and calf is necessary to maintain a productive dairy herd. We only allowed our newborns to stay with the dam for twenty-four hours. When a calf approaches its mother to nurse, it may bunt or lick the udder before beginning to suckle its choice of four teats. The calf's presence and preparation to nurse stimulate the release of the hormone oxytocin within the mother's bloodstream, which triggers the "letdown" of milk for the calf's meal. If the calf were allowed to remain with its dam over an extended period of time, it would stimulate the letdown of milk many times throughout the day, and her production would quickly decline to the needs of her calf. Because the cow produces much more milk than necessary to feed her baby, dairy farmers are in the business of selling her surplus. The goal is to stimulate the cow to let down her milk for the milking machine and produce as much milk as possible by removing all of it two or three times daily. This habit must be established early by removing her calf shortly after birth.

In this particular case, Jill's calf had already established how much milk he needed from Jill, and her production had started to decline to match those needs. However, not long after we separated them, Jill began to increase production to help meet our needs — filling the milk tank to pay the bills.

After Brad left, Ron, the boys, and I went to the pasture to catch Jill's calf. The calf eyed us suspiciously, blinked, and then looked back at the woods.

"Think it's a heifer?" I asked.

"Quite big for a heifer," Ron said, "but then, Jill's a big cow, too, and the calf is probably a week old, so I suppose it could be."

As we drew nearer, the baby blatted, "*bla-a-a, bla-a-a,*" then turned and bolted in the direction of its hiding place. We gave chase and moved in close enough to surround it. Ron secured his arms around its neck. As it hopped around, I reached under the rear legs, hoping to feel four small teats. Instead, I felt a sack.

"A bull," I said, disappointedly.

Not yet ready to meet people after his week of freedom, the calf hopped along, just out of reach, as the boys ran beside him.

"He's playing tag with us," Kyle said. Each time we came near, he trotted away again, getting ever closer to the barn.

"I think he's looking for his mother," Travis said.

Sure enough, Jill watched out the window as we brought her baby closer to the barn. She bellowed at him and he blatted in return. After a short reunion with his mother inside the barn, he was taken to the nursery.

"Daddy, can we keep him?" Kyle begged. "Don't send him away on the cattle truck. He's so pretty and I've already named him Alex."

"I guess we could raise him," Ron said. "Jill is our best cow; maybe we could use him to breed the heifers when he's old enough."

Jill's secret delivery and ability to hide her calf for an entire week was a stunning and humbling lesson. From that time on, whenever we had a cow to deliver, we remembered Jill's clever trick and kept the pregnant cow inside the barn where we could keep an eye on her.

THE COWS ARE OUT!

Six

Feeding a Newborn: A Test of Wills

When I see beef cattle grazing in a pasture with mothers nursing their young, I know that Mother Nature is pleased. Beef farmers do it the way she intended, with mother and calf together.

Since the whole point of dairy farming is to have cows produce at full capacity, calves are separated from their mothers and fed their mother's thick, yellow colostrum in pails. Some farmers feed calves milk from a large nipple bottle. It's quick and easy. However, when we bought our farm, Uncle Albert told us that bottle-feeding calves only reinforces their sucking instinct and can have disastrous results later. After bottle-fed calves are weaned and grouped by age in pens or in a pasture, they may instinctively continue to suck each other's small teats, causing permanent damage to undeveloped udders. This is a habit that is practically impossible to break.

Feeding a newborn calf from a pail is what I needed to do, even though it is contrary to Mother Nature's plan in a number of ways. A calf naturally reaches up toward the dam's teat; I wanted her head down in a pail. A calf prefers to suckle a teat; I wanted her to suck the milk directly. A calf bunts the dam's udder to stimulate milk letdown; instead, she bunts my milk pail, barks my shins, and spills the milk. If Mother Nature had her way, a calf would nurse small amounts of milk many times during the day and night; I offered larger portions in my pail just twice daily.

Although I eventually taught most newborns to drink from a pail, Mother Nature always had the last laugh.

If there were a uniform for feeding calves, it might include a wet suit, taped hands, shin guards, an athletic cup for males, and steel-toed shoes. The process was usually the same. It took one person to hold the pail and another to persuade the calf to drink. While a helper held the pail of warm colostrum, I straddled the newborn, inserted one hand in the calf's mouth, scooped up some milk with my other hand, and splashed it onto her tongue. With luck, after she tasted the milk she'd suck my fingers. I would then slowly lower my hand, hoping she'd follow

I am trying to show off a newborn heifer for a photo as part of registering it with the Holstein-Friesian Association of America.

it into the pail of milk. That usually didn't happen immediately. Instead, since my fingers gave no milk, she bunted my hand against the inside of the pail, slopping milk on my shirtsleeves. I would scoop more milk into the calf's mouth and she would suck my fingers enthusiastically until she thrust her head up again. I would firmly push her head into the pail and she would gulp a mouthful of milk. As she slurped, I tried to ease my fingers from her mouth. More often than not she would grab them and slam my hand against the pail, her razor-sharp bottom teeth slitting my fingers. By then, most of the milk had slopped into my boot anyway. As I stood to relieve my back, she would bunt my leg and suck my pants. As my patience waned, I would seize her nose and shove it to the bottom of the pail. She would register her objection by stomping on my toes. In the process of stomping on me, her head would bump the pail handle and spill the remaining milk into the sawdust. I would leave her bunting the side of the pen while I went to refill my pail.

I always knew that Mother Nature was chuckling.

I remember one newborn calf that gave me a particularly hard time. When I entered her pen, she seemed anxious to try it my way. She sucked my fingers heartily as I lowered my hand into the pail. When the pail was empty she wanted more, but I yanked it away and hastily retreated from the pen.

The next morning, I decided to feed her first and get it over with. When I set the pail down to climb over the side of the pen, the clang of the handle brought a chorus of wails from the nursery. The new calf trotted toward me, only to back away when I tried to straddle her. "Yes," I said to her, "I shoved your nose to the bottom of the pail yesterday."

I scooped and splashed milk into her mouth, but she refused to lower her head. She sucked my fingers, but became

47

impatient when they produced no milk. She bunted my hand and stepped into the pail, dumping its contents onto my clean pants. "You can just wait for your breakfast," I said crossly, pulling my soaked pants away from my leg. "You can wait until after I feed the others."

When I entered the nursery again with two full pails, the calves eagerly lined up with their heads through the pen gates. One calf stretched her neck and sucked her tongue while others bunted the air, anticipating their milk. As the first calf drank I braced myself against the pail because she had never gotten over bunting. The second heifer drank slowly because she sucked her tongue as she drank. The third still needed my finger as a reminder that she must put her head down to get her milk. As soon as the pail was empty, up came her head again. The last three gulped their milk, then sucked the nose of the calf beside them. Like unsatisfied bottle babies who suck their thumbs, the pail-fed calves spent the next few minutes sucking their own tongues, each other's noses, or the handle of the pen door.

I returned to my problem child with a fresh pail of milk. By this time she was so hungry that she quickly took my finger and followed it into the pail. When the milk was nearly gone, I carefully slipped my hand away and she continued sucking the imaginary teat. Satisfied that I had won, I tried to pull the empty pail away. The calf dove to the bottom for more milk so I slid the pail from under her nose and hustled to the side of the pen. Still not satisfied, she chased the pail, licking and butting it. I stepped up onto the rail of the pen and bent to drop the pail over the side. It was then that the newborn took full advantage of my position and bunted her hardest yet.

By that point, Mother Nature was probably no longer chuckling — she must have been in the middle of a real belly laugh.

SEVEN

Old Frank Davis

Long before I actually met him, I heard about old Frank
Davis. During college Ron and I passed his shack when we
visited Ron's grandparents, John and Carrie Ingraham, at Gold
Top Farm on Knox Ridge. We automatically looked in the
direction of Frank's outhouse, which faced the road. You see,
Frank never wanted to miss anything, so he never closed the
outhouse door. If Frank was on schedule when we happened by,
we couldn't help seeing him sitting there, drawers dropped to
the floor around his ankles.

Ron got to know Frank when Ron worked summers for his
grandfather. The local farmers hired Frank to weed corn and
clean out chicken houses.

"Allan [Ron's cousin] and I and the other boys used to play
tricks on Frank when we weeded corn," Ron said. "That was
before there were herbicides to kill the weeds so we weeded the
corn by hand. A crew of seven or eight started at one end of the
field and each weeded a row at a time. We filled grain bags with
the weeds we pulled and when the bags were full, we lugged
them to the rock wall to empty them. Each worker marked his

row of corn by dropping his hat at the end of the row. When Frank put his hat down, one of the boys would steal it so that he couldn't find it when he came back. Frank would wander up and down the field trying to find the row he had been weeding."

"But you never stole Frank's hat, did you?" I asked.

"I'm sorry to say now that, yes, I did," Ron confessed.

"Did you ever give it back to him?"

"Well, while Frank was looking for his hat on the edge of the field, one of us snuck back out and dropped it at the end of another row. After he found it we'd hear him mutter and see the corn rustle as he searched for the spot where he'd left off weeding. Of course, he never found the spot because we always put his hat by a different row. Good thing Grampa didn't find out what we were doing. He'd have tanned our hides."

Ron's mother, Alcadia, remembers when her mother, Carrie, made dinner for all the workers, including Frank, while he was there to clean out their chicken house. She told me that Frank never took off his soiled hat and never spoke at the table except when he needed food.

"Bread," he growled.

"Say please," Alcadia said.

"Bread," he repeated.

"Frank, can't you say please?" she coaxed.

"*Bread*," Frank growled louder, staring at the plate of homemade slices.

"Pass him the bread, Alcadia," said John, her father. "What difference does it make if he says please?"

"He should have some table manners," she insisted.

"It's too late for that," John said. Frank impatiently wiped his knife on the slice of bread.

"Butter," he growled.

"Did I hear you say please?" Alcadia asked, turning her ear toward him.

"Butter," Frank repeated, not taking his eyes off the plate of butter.

"Say please, Frank," Alcadia asked as she picked up the butter dish and held it for a moment.

"*Butter.*"

John chuckled as she reluctantly passed Frank the butter.

"When I was a little fellow," Ron said, "Frank drove a touring car. He chewed tobacco and spit out the window as he rode along. Trouble is he didn't always remember to roll down the window! And in the winter when it was too cold to roll down the window, he used the side pockets on the door for a spittoon."

I remember the day I finally met Frank on one of our regular visits to Knox Ridge. We were invited to Uncle Albert and Aunt Lona's for dinner. They lived just up the road from Albert's parents, John and Carrie. We were never actually introduced because everyone else sitting at Aunt Lona's dinner table already knew Frank and he wasn't the sort of person who needed a formal introduction. I would have recognized him even if Uncle Albert hadn't said, "Here comes Frank Davis walking down the road."

"Oh, no!" said Aunt Lona, scraping back her chair and hurrying out of the room.

"Where is she going?" Ron asked. Albert shrugged.

Lona returned carrying a straight chair, which she placed in the middle of the living room floor, well back from and facing the dining table. "I hope he has already eaten dinner," Lona said as she quickly spread a sheet of plastic over the seat of the chair.

"Is Frank that dirty?" I whispered to Ron.

"Quite grotty," Ron said.

Lona met Frank as he approached the back door. "Hello, Frank, come in," she said cheerfully. "We're just finishing dinner. I have a chair for you in the living room."

She led him in and pointed to the chair. I tried not to stare, but this was my first close-up look at the town eccentric – a fixture in many Maine towns in those days. I caught an unpleasant whiff of his unwashed body and clothes as he shuffled by the table. His stringy hair stuck out from under his hat, which looked as though it were permanently affixed to his head. The pockets of his tattered jacket sagged, and I was sure he slept in his clothes. His steely eyes peered through bushy eyebrows and scraps of recent meals clung to his beard. Frank accepted the chair and sat down facing us.

"Nice day," Albert remarked. Frank nodded.

"Ronald and Trudy are here for a visit," Lona added. Frank nodded.

"I haven't seen you for some time, Frank," Ron said. Frank nodded. "Have you cleaned out any chicken houses lately?"

Frank scowled and stared at Albert.

"Frank tells me that he can't get many jobs now," Albert said. "The farmers say he's too slow, but he can't understand that because he says he's just as tired at the end of the day as he always was." He smiled at us and then looked at Frank. "Isn't that right, Frank? You get just as tired as you did when you were a young fellow." Frank nodded fervently.

"How about a cigar, Frank. Had a smoke lately?" Albert asked. Frank straightened in his chair and watched as Albert went to the drawer, found a cigar, and handed it to him. Frank unwrapped the cigar and stroked it, then sniffed while sliding it slowly back and forth under his nose. He slipped the cigar into his mouth, rolling it as he licked it, then held it up for inspection. Finally, he puckered his lips and sucked the cigar out of sight.

I looked at Ron in disbelief. Lona cleared her throat. "Albert," she said in a hushed voice, "does he smoke?"

"Darned if I know," Albert chuckled. After extracting the cigar from his mouth, Frank bit off the tip end and began to nibble on it. "Let me help you with a light," Albert said. He reached to the top cupboard shelf and pulled down a box of wooden matches. Frank leaned forward as Albert struck the match that ignited a three-inch flame and held it up to the end of the cigar. As I watched Frank suck on the cigar, I hoped that the flame wouldn't light his beard, too.

"That's it, Frank, take two or three good puffs to be sure it's lit in good shape," Albert urged. Frank inhaled for an extraordinarily long time. We all held our breath waiting for him to exhale. Finally, Frank's cheeks puffed out and he blew both the cigar and smoke out of his mouth. He leaned his elbows on his knees, coughing and sputtering.

"Albert, for heaven's sake!" Lona scolded. "He'll be sick!"

"Take it easy, Frank," Albert advised, patting him on the back, "better go a little slower."

Lona and I busied ourselves in the kitchen while Frank worked on his cigar. After cigar smoke filled the house, Albert ushered Frank toward the door. "It's been nice seeing you, Frank," Albert said. "Better save the other half of that cigar for another time."

There was no hiding everyone's relief when Frank left. As soon as he went by the kitchen window, Lona hurried back to the living room and removed the plastic from the chair.

"Do you always put plastic on the chair when Frank visits?" Ron asked.

"Except for the first time," she replied, "and I was glad that I hadn't offered him our best chair. After he left, I found a big grease spot on the cushion."

"What was it?" Ron asked.

"It seems that Frank takes a lot of mineral oil," Lona explained.

"Yeah, so?" Ron quizzed.

"Enough so that it runs right on through," Lona declared.

"No wonder he spends so much time in the outhouse," Ron remarked.

EIGHT

Cousin Leland

The phone rang. I was sure it was Ron's cousin Leland because he usually called right at breakfast time. I had come from the barn ahead of Ron, but it would be useless for me to answer the call. Leland would want to talk to Ron. He always wanted Ron.

"Hello, Trudy? Ronald there? No? Well, I'll call back, then."

"I could give him a message," I would say.

"Well, no, I think I'll call back."

I had fixed Ron's breakfast: orange juice; scrambled eggs; toast; three kinds of dry cereal mixed together in a mixing bowl and topped with sliced bananas and ample cream; and a tall glass of milk. Breakfast is Ron's favorite meal. He doesn't eat before starting the half-past-three morning milking, so by the time he comes to breakfast, he has already done almost a full day's work by most folks' standards.

"Leland called," I said, as Ron came through the back hallway.

"We must have a heifer in heat down at his place," he said.

Leland was Ron's distant cousin and he lived less than a mile away. In Leland's old barn, where he and his father had milked cows for many years, he took care of a dozen or more of our heifers that were of breeding age but had not yet given birth. After Leland's father died in the 1950s, Leland continued to keep a milking herd until 1961 when bulk tank storage replaced ten-gallon milk cans. Leland wasn't willing to make the financial investment necessary to meet the new requirements, so he sold his cows and stopped shipping milk to the dairy.

Several years after Leland went out of business, we bought his property, which included his house and ten acres of land, using another loan from FHA. (While it was hard to get money from FHA to buy a farm, once you owned a farm, it was very easy to get more to run it!) Leland wanted to remain active during his retirement years, so he agreed to house and care for our heifers if we provided the necessary grain, hay and bedding. In return for his labor, we gave him a lifetime lease on his house and an adequate supply of fresh milk for himself and his cats.

The phone rang again before we had finished breakfast. This time Ron answered.

"Hello, Ronald?" Leland said. "You have a heifer down here with a juicy snapper."

The description of events was always the same: "I mooed at her and she mooed back at me. She licks me when I walk by her, and when I stand in front of her, she tries to ride me."

"I'll be down to breed her later. Thank you, Leland."

"Ayuh."

"Let me guess," I said, after Ron hung up the phone. I mimicked Leland's whiny voice. " 'You have a heifer down here with a juicy snapper' — am I right? Why won't he tell me that?"

"I suppose he's embarrassed," Ron said. "He's from the old school when women were escorted to the house when the cow was brought to the bull for breeding."

Ron's mother was born and brought up on the family dairy farm, yet she never witnessed a mating. In that era, women were not involved with such acts as breeding a heifer. That was men's work.

Men's work, men's talk! I thought. Could Leland possibly think that I didn't know about juicy snappers? No, of course not. He sees me when I go to his place with Ron to help insemi-nate the heifers with frozen semen and a plastic rod. But he makes himself scarce. If I were not there with Ron, Leland would go to the barn to watch, help, and chat.

When the phone rang in the morning, I was tempted to pick it up and say, "Leland, do we have a heifer down at your place with a juicy snapper?" But I couldn't imagine Leland's reaction. Would he hang up on me? Would he avoid me forever? I contin-ued to play the game, because I didn't want to shock or embarrass an old man who was long an important part of the family.

After his own parents died, Leland visited Ron's Grammie and Grampa Ingraham every week. Leland and Grampa were first cousins and had lots to talk about. After they discussed their current health problems, they moved on to recent deaths around the county. Eventually the conversation turned to farm-ing. Leland related Ron's progress with haying and estimated how many bales had been put up for the heifers in his care. Grampa, in turn, updated Leland on the happenings at Gold Top Farm that his son, John Jr., now operated with the help of his four sons.

Although retired, Grampa's human alarm clock was forever set to half past three. Each morning he arose and slowly made his way to the barn to observe how many cows were milked, how much milk was shipped to the dairy, which fields were mowed, and, most important of all, to see if the hired man was performing his chores satisfactorily.

Ron visited Grampa Ingraham regularly, too. They usually sat in the den with Grampa at his big rolltop desk. He would ask Ron how farming was going and Ron always said, "Good."

And Grampa would often answer back, "You know, *no* Ingraham has ever had his name in the town report for unpaid taxes. You're half Ingraham and that goes for you, too."

"It'll never happen," Ron would reply.

"Let me know if you need help," Grampa said. "And remember, if you can keep your troubles in the barn, you'll do just fine."

One time, Ron reminded him of some help from the past. "Remember when Trudy and I used to visit you on weekends while we were at the University? You always let me fill the tank of the '50 Ford with farm gas."

"Oh," Grampa said with a chuckle. "I wished that little blue car could talk. I bet it could've told me some stories."

One afternoon, Ron's Grammie saw Leland's green pickup truck come up the long driveway, so she set an extra place at the dinner table. Grampa, who liked to keep a close watch on the outdoors from his armchair, was already hobbling toward the door. "Come in, Leland. Take off your coat and sit down."

Even though she and Grampa were alone in the big farmhouse, Grammie still prepared lots of food. She had cooked dinner for countless people — family, hired help, salesmen, and friends — for years. She was always ready to serve guests and Grampa loved visitors, especially at dinnertime. Anyone who stopped by the farm at dinnertime received an invitation to join them.

Alcadia, my mother-in-law, told me that as a young girl growing up in that household, two of the reasons she vowed never to marry a farmer were that "you never knew what time to plan a meal, and you never knew how many people were coming to eat it."

On this day, Leland was the only guest. "You'll stay to dinner, of course," Grampa said. His invitations were hard to refuse.

"Think I'll leave my coat on," Leland drawled, "but I guess I could stay to dinner. Sure you have enough, Carrie?"

"Aplenty; come to the table." Grammie walked stiffly to the dining room, permanently stooped from years of lugging heavy pails of milk from the barn to the milk room. When she was unable to perform that chore, a cart with wheels was built to replace her.

"Carrie, pass Leland the meat!" Grampa bellowed, noticing that Leland didn't have any meat on his plate.

"Can't chew that, John, thanks just the same. I'll have some gravy on my potatoes and a piece of Carrie's good homemade bread, though."

"Leland, why don't you get yourself a set of teeth so you can eat some decent food? What do you eat besides oatmeal and baked beans?"

Grampa already knew the answer, but he loved to prod.

"I eat what agrees with me," Leland said. "Besides, I hear that false teeth are expensive."

"Now, Leland, I know you can afford to buy some false teeth. What you need is a good thick piece of beefsteak to put some color in your cheeks."

A twinkle came to Grampa's eyes.

"Leland, where's your life? Your *oomph*?" Grampa demanded.

Leland was an enigma to Grampa, who was a man who lived his life fully with hard work and hard play, loved his wife and four children, and partook of hearty food and drink. He had been a progressive, successful farmer and businessman, well-known and respected throughout the county. He worked hard, maintained a well-kept, neat farm, and was dedicated to both community service and his family.

Grampa found it difficult to understand his cousin who had grown up an only child and lived with his parents until their deaths. Leland, also a retired dairy farmer, was a reclusive bachelor. He could afford the comforts of life, yet he deprived himself of basics such as indoor plumbing, central heat, clothes (except for absolute necessities), and now, even a basic food group because he would not spend the money to buy false teeth.

But for Leland, his religion had taught him that earthly life is a temporary misery, to be endured until death, when all things are made well and beautiful.

Each time Grampa thought of Leland and his sacrifices, he was vividly reminded of the sharp contrast in their lifestyles. Grampa had memorized what he called "Leland's list," and loved to draw it out of Leland. It was a conversation that became a well-known ritual.

"Leland," he would begin slowly, "how far away from home you ever been?"

"Thirty miles to South Union to visit my mother's people."

"Ever stay away overnight?"

"Nope."

"Ever eat out in a restaurant?"

"Nope, never eat in public."

"Ever been to the movies?"

"Nope."

"Ever had a smoke or a chew?"

"Nope."

"Ever had a drink?"

"Nope."

Grampa shook his head from side to side. Grammie, who also knew the list well, fumbled with her silverware and looked down at her plate.

"Leland, have you ever danced with a woman?"

"Nope."

"Have you ever slept with a woman?"

"Nope."

"Damn, Leland, you're dead already!"

THE COWS ARE OUT!

NINE

Ruts

The morning air smelled of spring mud. The sky above was clear blue, but on the horizon it got paler, almost white, as the sun climbed over the distant ridge. Living on Knox Ridge allowed us to enjoy sunrises on the house side of the farm and sunsets behind the milk room and barn. I looked out through the milk room window and studied the ruts made by the milk truck that had sunk into the mud of our spongy driveway where frost inched its way to the surface.

Ruts! Oh, they so vividly brought back the memory of the ruts I made in the field one wet summer — ruts big enough for me to lie down in and hide. Ruts big enough to put my marriage and my dedication to farming to the test. Ruts that brought to the surface the stress caused by long hours and hard work.

I had hoped for dry summers ever since.

When we first began farming, baled hay was the only forage we grew, and before we had much hired help, it was my chore to bale. Hay is "made" in late afternoon, at exactly the same time that the afternoon milking has to be done. I should have learned to milk the cows instead of doing field work, but I had followed a friendly neighbor's advice. Shortly after we moved to the farm, Margaret called on me. "It's none of my business," she began, "but I have a piece of advice for you. Don't learn to milk! The men can always find other things to do and after a while you'll find yourself doing all the milking."

"You'll have to bale while I go milk," Ron had said, "but the field has some problem spots. There's a wet hole just ten or twelve windrows from the edge. You'll be able to tell when you get to it."

"I can see it from here," I said, looking toward the long rows of dried cut hay waiting to be baled.

"Just go around it and leave the hay there — that's better than getting stuck," he advised. "The other spot is close to where those bushes meet the field on the lower side."

"I think I know where that one is, too," I said confidently.

He hooked the hay trailer to the baler and added new twine to the compartment in the back while the boys watched me start the tractor and baler. "You boys help Daddy with the chores and we'll go get a milkshake later," I said.

"Stay away from the wet spots," Ron shouted one more time over the noise of the machines. I nodded and waved. Balers seem to perform better with someone watching, especially a mechanically inclined person. But that day, luck was with me as I went it alone — it tied bale after bale with ease and kicked them onto the trailing wagon. The trailer was almost full as I neared the wet hole that Ron had warned me about. One more time around and I would have to change trailers. Going down-hill I figured I could bale one more windrow before going around the wet place. It didn't even look wet from my perspective. It must have been dry enough to mow and rake over; I decided to chance one more row. It was a mistake. Soon the tractor slowed and began to sink. As I increased the throttle, the huge rear wheels began to spin. I stopped, turned off the baler, and tried to back up. The wheels spun, sank deeper, and the baler started to jackknife. My face flushed. Oh, no, what will Ron say now?

I jumped down and unhooked the trailer, hoping to move the tractor and baler ahead without its weight. But stuck is stuck. Even without the full trailer, every attempt I made to move the tractor caused its wheels to dig deeper ruts into the earth. I turned off the key. I knew what my next move had to be, but I dreaded telling Ron. I put the words together in my head as I walked toward the road. "I have bad news for you . . ." No, I'll be more positive: "I've baled one trailer full . . ." No, he'll wonder why I'm back so soon. "I'm sorry, but . . ." I reluctantly headed down over the hill to the farm.

Ron looked up from beside a cow as I entered the barn. I walked slowly to him and didn't look directly at him. "Guess what I did?" I asked, holding my breath.

"Are you done already?" he asked.

"No, I'm stuck!"

"You're what?" he bellowed.

"That's right, I'm stuck, right where you told me not to go. I'm sor—"

"I ought to kick your ass," he threatened.

"What?" I stared at him, completely bewildered. In our eight years of marriage, he had never spoken to me this way. I was hoping for understanding, sympathy, help. Instead, I was totally crushed. I turned on my heels and stormed off. "Bale your own hay!" I shouted over my shoulder.

"If you can't hold up your end of this deal, you'd *better* leave," he yelled back.

His second verbal blow was harder than the first. Tears burned my eyelids. Leave — yes, that's just what I'll do! I thought. We'll see how long he can do it by himself. I ran to the house and up to the attic room to find my suitcase. Tears streamed into my mouth. I threw open the suitcase and blindly reached into my dresser drawers for clothes, any clothes within reach. I fumbled handfuls into the suitcase. I'll show him, I thought, now sobbing aloud. We'll see if he can bale hay and milk cows at the same time. And I'll leave him with two little boys to take care of, and all the cooking and housework. Hold up my end, eh? He can *have* my end. I threw my suitcase into the backseat of the car and started the engine. As I backed from the garage, the boys ran out of the barn.

"Where are you going, Mommy?" Kyle asked.

"I don't know!" I blurted, and roared out of the driveway.

I drove like a robot, trembling with hurt and anger. After my anguish subsided a bit, I wondered where I was headed. I know, I thought; I'll go to Bangor to see Ron's parents and tell them what a crud he is, how mean he was to me, how I tried to help bale hay and he bellowed at me after I made a mistake. Yes, I'll tell them what a cruel and hateful son they raised. I wiped my face and ran my fingers through my damp and dirty hair. My jeans were stained and my arms and hands were grimy. I smoothed my blouse and glanced in the rearview mirror at my red and swollen eyes.

I drove into my in-laws' driveway. No one was home, no one to tell my troubles. I cried again. Did Ron really mean it? I was quite certain he wouldn't kick me. It was just a figure of speech, uttered out of frustration at not being able to leave the cows and pull the tractor out, at me doing exactly what he had told me not to do. No, he wouldn't kick me, but it was his telling me to leave that upset me so.

I decided to keep on going north to Aroostook County, to where home really was, to my parents who would listen and understand. I backed the car into the street and drove away from Bangor. I looked at the gas gauge — it was nearing empty. I reached for my purse and pulled out my wallet. Three dollars! I gasped. That won't buy enough gas to get me to Lincoln, forget Caribou.

I continued driving aimlessly around Bangor, and then drove back to my in-laws'. Still no sign of them. While I sat waiting for them, I began to wonder if they would sympathize with me. Maybe they would side with their son. I realized that I couldn't stay there. I had no place to go but back to the farm.

I drove back slowly, thinking of the boys. They had looked so worried when I left. And, I had promised them milkshakes.

When I arrived, the cows had been milked and were out to pasture. No one was around. I drove to the field where I had left the stuck tractor and baler. It was now unstuck and Ron was baling the remaining hay. When the boys saw me, they ran to the car.

"Where did you go, Mommy?" Kyle asked.

"Daddy said you were mad at him," Travis added.

"Get into the car," I said, "we're going to get milkshakes."

When we returned from the diner, Ron was standing in the shed doorway.

"You came back," he said.

"How far could I go on three dollars?" I asked. "What did you think I would do?"

"I'm sorry," he said, "I shouldn't have said those things. I thought you really were leaving for good, and then when you came back and got the boys, I thought you were taking them with you. I'm glad you're all back. Where did you go?"

"We went to the diner to get milkshakes — three small and one large," I said as I handed him his. Chocolate, extra thick.

THE COWS ARE OUT!

TEN

The Cows Are Out!

"**M**OO-OO-OO!"

I lifted my head from the pillow so that my left ear could verify what I thought the right one had heard. Then, tilting my head toward the open bedroom window on my side of the bed, I heard the scuffing of hooves on the driveway.

"*Moo-oo-oo!*"

"Damn!" I half whispered.

"What?" came a faint voice from Ron's side of the bed. "What did you say?"

"The cows are out!"

I ran to the window and peered into the darkest night of summer. I couldn't see anything, but I could hear the cows shuffling, running. The excited, high-pitched moos, different from the moos of confined cows, seemed to be saying: "We're out where we shouldn't be. Isn't this fun?"

I ran down the stairs, Ron at my heels. No time to waste. Every second that cows taste freedom means destruction to the lawn, garden, and fields. I pulled on my Tingley boots, knowing from past experience that every step at night among a herd of cows is an adventure. We both grabbed flashlights from the kitchen windowsill.

"How did they get out?" I asked.

"Probably someone left the gate down — whoever did chores last night — whoever let the cows out to pasture," Ron said.

"Damn," I said for a second time that night.

When I opened the shed door I saw four or five tails, straight up in the air, as the cows rounded the corner of the house and moved onto the front lawn.

Years ago I gave up trying to have a smooth front lawn like I'd seen in pictures. Some people look for a robin or crocuses or pussy willows as the first sign of spring. I look for new holes on the front lawn. The first time the cows ran across the spongy front lawn, I thought that it was an unlikely accident, so I filled in the four-inch-deep hoofprints and sprinkled grass seed on top. If I had continued the practice, our lawn would be a collage of patched hoofprints. Although the holes aren't obvious to someone passing by, or even from the kitchen window, every time I mowed the front lawn I was reminded to step carefully lest I fall into one and sprain my ankle.

"You keep them coming around the front of the house," Ron instructed, "and I'll go around back and head them off at the driveway."

As I trotted behind the cows that had just passed the shed door, I heard coughing and panting behind me. My flashlight illuminated more cows coming in my direction, so I stepped aside until they caught up with the others. By the time I reached the front lawn, the cows had gone beyond the driveway and into the road. Ron had not reached the end of the driveway in time to stop them.

"Where are you?" I shouted.

"I'm on the side of the road, trying to get in front of them."

"What can I do?"

"Stay there, maybe I can turn them around." Ron ran beside the cows, but the faster he ran, the faster they ran. We were lucky there was no traffic. When the clattering of hooves on the tar grew fainter, I realized that they must be nearing the top of the hill. The clattering stopped.

They've left the road, I thought. If they turned right, they'd be in our hay field. Ron was on their right, so they probably turned left into a driveway where there had once been an old house and barn. I caught a glimpse of his flashlight to the left of the road. Ron knew about the old cellar hole there, but the cows did not. I pictured the whole herd falling in, breaking legs, panicking, and becoming trapped. Should I go help? I wondered. How can he possibly get all those cows headed back this way? If I leave, there won't be anyone to help on this end, to guide them back toward the barnyard. I remembered that cows at night, like cats, seem to be able to see where they're going. They dodge clotheslines and fence wire, although never, of course, the row of new peas in the garden. I decided I should worry more about Ron falling into the cellar hole than the cows.

I walked partway up the road, stopped, waited, and listened. In the distance I heard Ron's voice: "Get out of there! Move, you hammerheads — turn around — *git*!"

I felt helpless.

I paced on the tar, the Tingleys slapping my bare calves and my yellow nightie fluttering in the warm night breeze. At that moment, I resolved to check the gates myself every night before going to bed. I heard the clattering of hooves again in the distance, so I ran back to the end of the driveway and waited. I gazed at the dark, moonless sky. I reached up to touch it. There was not a star in sight.

Then I heard what sounded like a stampede coming back down the road toward me, a lot faster than they had left. It got louder and closer. Ron shouted from behind the cows, "Head them off at the driveway, Trude!"

"Okay, okay," I assured him.

"Use your flashlight to head them off at the driveway."

My flashlight? What good is my flashlight when forty cows are running straight at me? I waved the light and danced around in the road.

"Whoa. Whoa," I screamed, "*Whoa!*"

I still hadn't decided whether to stay in the middle of the road or dive into the ditch at the last second. Then I noticed lights shining behind me and turned to see a vehicle coming down our road. As it came closer, so did the cows. I waved my flashlight. Please see me, I prayed. The vehicle slowed and I saw a red, flashing light rotating on top of our neighbor's wrecker. With lights flashing, Earl stopped in the middle of the road by the end of the driveway and stepped out. I ran to his side as the cows turned into the driveway and went back through the open gate into the barnyard. Ron secured the gate and came back to the road where Earl and I were standing.

"Thanks a lot, Earl," Ron said breathlessly.

"That's all right," Earl said. "I saw the flashlight and wondered what was happening, so I came on over."

I stepped forward to give Earl a hug and a kiss. Then I looked down at my yellow nightie and boots, looked back at Earl, and ran for the house.

ELEVEN

Growing Up Fast: Farm-Style

Children grow up faster on a farm. By the age most children are riding bicycles, our sons, Kyle and Travis, could drive. They began by sitting on their father's lap, learning to steer and shift gears on the tractor. As soon as their legs grew long enough to reach the clutch and brake, they began raking and tedding hay. Learning to drive cars and trucks came easily after that.

Both of our sons also became adept at building mainte-nance, from simple carpentry jobs to helping build a barn ell addition. They never received toy tools as Christmas presents because they were mini-mechanics with real tools as soon as they could hold them in their hands. They learned the simple but innovative plumbing and electrical skills required to run a farm because farmers can't always afford professional assistance or take time to drive twenty miles for parts.

Then there's the work ethic. Farm children learn young what a day's work is and the importance of completing tasks. It may be the routine of barn chores or troubleshooting a broken machine and thinking out a solution to repair it. With so many

Travis (on the left) and Kyle after delivering a calf, 1977.

work demands, there is ample opportunity for the feeling of accomplishment.

Non-farming rural children also learn the work ethic and gain knowledge of gardening and nature.

When I was teaching school in the late 1960s, one of my third-grade students needed a place to live one summer because his mother was moving to Belfast to work in a chicken plant. Danny came to us with his pet, Peter Rabbit. It was the beginning of an eight-year span during which Danny lived with us off and on depending on his situation at home.

Danny shared his knowledge of birds, wildflowers and trees with Kyle and Travis, who were five and three years old at the time. He led the boys on nature walks and showed them his world. They built "cabins" among the rock walls of the pasture. One spring they collected thousands of violet blossoms and we

made violet syrup for topping pancakes and ice cream. We ate
the roots of day lilies. He devoted time to the family garden and
to harvesting, helping prepare and freeze vegetables. We learned
recycling from Danny.

Danny, of course, shared in the daily chores and learned
about dairy farming. The lessons were many, as most people,
even those who grow up near farms, don't know the details of a
dairy farm. Cows are vegetarians and have four stomachs. They
eat huge amounts of hay or grass that go into the first two
stomachs. Cows usually lie down to rest and process food. Hay
or grass is chewed, swallowed and regurgitated, and then
chewed more slowly a second time before being swallowed
again. When you see cows lying out in the pasture chewing
their cuds, you might think they are being lazy, but they are
actually working very hard to digest their food and make milk.
A cow has to pump four hundred pounds of blood through her
udder to make one pound of milk.

After cows are milked, the warm milk is cooled to thirty-
eight degrees and stored in a big stainless steel tank. A truck
comes every other day to pick it up and take it to the dairy
where it will be pasteurized and put into containers. From there,
the milk is taken to stores and supermarkets.

Farm children also learn to take on responsibilities at a young
age. One summer we had guests help us with the haying. The
adults all had reserved tickets to Lakewood Theater in Skowhegan,
but when it came time to leave, the haying wasn't done. Our
guests were appalled that we were going to leave the children to
finish baling and unloading the hay. We finally convinced them
that our boys were capable and proud to finish the haying.

Farm children gain respect for Mother Nature and learn
how to deal with her power and unpredictable ways. They learn

frustration when the rains come and soak hay that you have worked on for days mowing, tedding and raking. And they learn the pain of witnessing the death of a favorite calf and other life events that don't always turn out as you would like.

Another benefit of raising our two sons on a farm was that we didn't have to tell them the facts of life. When we made our decision to buy a dairy farm, we considered the many benefits and opportunities for them. We were aware of obvious pluses: a healthy outdoor environment, opportunities to care for pets and farm animals and take responsibility for their well-being. But it wasn't until later that the value of sex education provided by farm animals became evident.

It's not as easy as it used to be for farm children to learn those facts of life. When we first started farming, we had a bull on the premises to breed heifers in the pasture during summer and fall. The bull was also used to breed cows that didn't settle by artificial insemination. Having a bull in residence gave the boys an opportunity to observe mating in cattle, understand the reasons for it, and see a baby calf born nine months later. Transferring that understanding to other animals and people seemed natural. We were glad that we didn't have to explain the facts of life, and it was interesting to observe how their understanding of it developed.

When our son Kyle was in junior high, our hired worker's wife was pregnant with her first baby.

"The baby is supposed to arrive the second week of January," Ron told the boys.

"On which day?" Kyle asked.

"I don't think they know for certain the exact day," Ron replied.

"Why not?" Kyle persisted.

"Well ...," Ron started slowly, "people don't write those things down on a breeding chart like farmers do with cows." Kyle mulled that over for several minutes while all was silent around the supper table. Then he looked up at his father. "That often, huh?"

Another time when my parents were visiting us from The County, we discussed a plan to rearrange the heifers in the barn because some had grown too large for the freestall area. The heifers were about six months old, and among them was a young bull that we were raising to sell.

Travis spoke up. "Dad, we need to move Victor, the bull, out of there, right away."

"Why is that?" Ron asked.

"Because he's starting to sniff."

Soon after that, we stopped keeping a bull because we found we could improve our herd genetics faster with artificial insemination. Using frozen semen from bull stud companies allowed us to use genetically superior bulls from all over the United States and Canada. The other reason we stopped keeping a bull was a matter of safety. After one year, a bull's disposition may change from friendly to aggressive. Unless a farm has an adequate place to contain a mature bull, it can be risky to keep one.

It was a relief to think that the sex education had been completed and that the boys were old enough to understand and talk openly with us about cows and people. Then down came my young nephews from The County to spend time with us during the summer. By this time, the bull was gone. What do I say when they ask if we have a bull? Do I show them the semen tank? I didn't look forward to my nephews' questions, but I knew there would be some because their only exposure to animals at that time was spayed cats.

The family — Travis, Brigette, Kyle, me, Evelyn, and Ron — poses for the 1978 holiday photo. Officially named Gold Top Evelyn Ann Cherry, Evelyn was 16 years old and the last remaining cow from when we bought the farm in 1966.

One afternoon, my nephew, Jody, stood by the maternity pen watching a cow give birth. He was particularly concerned because the calf was coming with difficulty. Ron pulled on the handles of the calving chains that held the calf's front feet while I eased the calf's head through the cow's vulva with my hands. The cow moaned as she strained. Jody's face showed his sympathy.

"Aunt T," Jody began, "it hurts, doesn't it?"

"Yes," I assured him, "it hurts."

"Do you think it's a heifer or a bull?" he asked.

"Probably a bull," I replied. "The head is huge."

"I hope it's a heifer so we can keep her," Jody said. "Aunt T, where's the calf's father?"

Oh, no, I thought, here come the questions. The sire, by artificial insemination, could be in California — but should I tell him that? I took the easy way out.

"Oh," I said, as matter-of-factly as I could, "the father is probably around the neighborhood somewhere." What a fib, I thought, waiting for the next question.

"Well," Jody said disgustedly, "he should be here!"

THE COWS ARE OUT!

Twelve

A Real Farmer's Tan

After we started farming, I was lucky if I made it to the beach once every year or two. Unfortunately, beach season coincides exactly with haying season, so if I wanted a tan, I had to get one while I worked.

I liked to rake with our old Farmall Super MD tractor because it had no modern canopy or cab to shade me. Its large, towel-covered seat was springy, and because the steering wheel had no slant, it left room to move, stretch my legs, prop them up on the headlight supports, or even stand while raking hay.

Usually, I wore shorts and sandals so my legs would tan nicely. For some reason on this particular day I felt an urge to really soak up the sunshine. I just needed the right moment.

After raking the outside windrow toward the inside of the field, I turned the rig around and raked the next row to the outside, combining the two. From there I continued on around the field, raking my way to the middle. Soon, I stood up and looked toward the road. Two fields and a birch-lined rock wall separated my field from the road, and I couldn't see any passing vehicles.

Surely no one would see me from this distance. I made my move. I stripped to the waist and hung my bra and tank top over the rear light. I was ready for a real tan.

Although pleased with my bold act, I didn't dare completely relax. Each time I rounded the corner that faced the direction of the road, I stood to watch for possible intruders. Sometimes the boys brought me a drink of water or a milkshake in mid-afternoon. I even imagined the sounds of approaching vehicles and estimated how quickly I could get dressed before they got close enough to see me. On the other hand, so what if they did see me? Ha! I thought. Here sits a girl who dressed and undressed in the closet during her first semester of college so that her roommate wouldn't see her naked. Now she's saying, so what?

Fortunately, I didn't have any company other than the sun as I raked the hay in solitude. By the time I had reached the middle of the field, I had soaked up ample sunshine for one day, so I reached down to the right of the tractor seat for my tank top and bra. They were gone! I frantically looked around. I searched the row of hay behind me. Nothing. The clothes must have bounced off the tractor when I hit a woodchuck hole. Never had a twenty-acre field looked so big; never had windrows of hay looked so long. I turned the tractor around to backtrack a bit. I stood as I drove, watching for my missing clothes as the rake turned over the rows of hay again. Even after I had re-raked several rows with no bra in sight, I decided I must continue looking. What choice did I have?

Each time I came around the field, I was sure that the lost items would appear in the next row. When only four rows remained, I had returned to the spot where I had begun my sunbathing. I couldn't rake that whole field a third time. I resigned myself to the loss.

Getting back from the field to the farm topless posed a problem because I had to drive a mile along the main road. I grabbed the towel that had protected my bare legs from the plastic-covered tractor seat, threw it over my shoulders, sat down on the edge of the field and waited. I figured by this time, Ron must be wondering what was taking me so long and would be along shortly to find out. Sure enough, in a short while, the pickup appeared. Holding the towel over my shoulders, I climbed into the truck.

"Don't even ask," I said to Ron before he could speak. "Just take me home and promise, not a word to a soul."

As he baled the hay the next day, Ron, too, watched for my lost clothes, but didn't have any better luck than I did.

Throughout the winter we joked as we opened the bales, hoping it would not be the hired boy who found my clothes bound up inside one of them.

Spring came and the cows went out to pasture. Soon they had the grass well trimmed down. Ron supplemented their diet with baled hay that he fed to them from a wagon parked in the back pasture. Cows who did not come to the barn at milking time could usually be found at the feed wagon stretching their necks and tongues to sweep up the remaining stems of hay.

One day at chore time, several cows remained at the wagon. Ron went to the back door of the barn and cupped his hands to his mouth. "Come, boss, come boss."

The cows looked in his direction, but stayed put. "I'll go down and drive them up," he said.

I watched as he walked down the lane, circled the wagon and urged the cows toward the barn. He climbed into the wagon, and grabbed the clump, shook it, and headed back. He grinned widely as he held the found articles high in the air, a tank top in one hand and a bra in the other.

"Lose something?" he shouted.

THIRTEEN

Cultivated Raspberries

One summer I discovered cultivated raspberries. I always knew they existed but I had never considered picking them, because for more than twenty years I had picked upwards of thirty quarts of wild raspberries in an abandoned pasture on our dairy farm.

Picking raspberries was one of the few legitimate reasons to avoid morning barn chores, so I took every opportunity to harvest my favorite of Mother Nature's berries.

Besides being more flavorful, wild raspberries were free. However, I paid dearly for their sweet, rare taste. I climbed over rock walls, tramped through bushes taller than I, stumbled over boulders and logs, and ducked tree branches. Once, I stepped into a woodchuck hole, fell, and spilled my pailful of berries. Another time, I reached for a handful of berries and put my hand into a hornet's nest. On another occasion, I was unaware of a mother bird on her nest. When I got too close for her comfort, she flew into my face and startled me so that I tipped my pail of berries onto the ground. These are just some of the reasons why wild raspberries are so precious.

Ron never picked more than a handful of raspberries in any given season, but he never failed to tell me when they were ripe. Heading out for his annual berry-checking excursion, he'd say he was going to check the fields to see if the second crop of hay was ready to cut; but I knew that the real reason was that his mouth watered for the first raspberry pie of the summer. He couldn't wait to announce that the raspberries were ripe so that I could pick them. One particular year when he told me they were ripe, I couldn't get to them right away. Even the mornings seemed too hot for picking, and then afternoon showers kept me away. By the time I made it to the patch, most of the berries were already gone. They had prematurely ripened under the intense summer heat and then were beaten off the bushes by the heavy afternoon showers. In addition, my competition — a bear — had already trampled his way through the bushes and taken more than his fair share.

I shared my raspberry patch with the bear for many years. Although I never saw him, I once heard him at the edge of the old pasture near the woods when he and I had decided to pick berries at the same time. He moved heavily, parting the bushes and snapping tree branches as he went. He stopped occasionally as if he were aware of my intrusion. I've been told that one should not run from a bear, so I didn't earnestly try to see him. I wasn't sure I had enough self-control to stay still. I continued picking nervously, hoping he'd notice or smell me and be more afraid of me than I was of him. After a while he crashed his way back into the woods.

On this day, it was dusk already and the paths through the bushes were fresh, so I was particularly nervous about the bear. I didn't even stop to taste the berries. Instead of filling my peanut butter pail, I hurriedly picked the few remaining berries and returned home before dark. After removing leaves, twigs, and worms, we had barely enough raspberries for our cereal the next morning.

"You didn't pick enough berries to put in the freezer for the traditional Christmas pie," Ron said.

"No," I replied. "If we want more, the only solution is to pick cultivated raspberries."

I decided to give it a try. When I arrived at Raven's Berry Farm the next day, there were people, no bears, and rows — straight rows! — of pruned raspberry bushes adorned with huge berries that practically leapt into my pail. I didn't have to climb over rock walls, boulders and logs, or duck tree branches. There were no woodchuck holes, hornets or nesting birds. I didn't even have to bend over. This was too easy. I moved along the cushioned, mowed aisles, and filled three pails in less time than it would have taken to fill one pail with wild berries. When I paid Julie, the price seemed unbelievably low for the large, perfectly shaped raspberries. After I arrived home, there were no twigs, leaves or worms to remove.

"Good pie," Ron remarked at supper.

I agreed.

After chores the next morning, we sat down to a breakfast of cereal, raspberries and cream.

"You know," I said to Ron, "I don't think I'll ever go back to my wild raspberry patch after picking cultivated berries. No sprained ankles, I'm not scratched or stung and I hardly felt tired."

We both took a mouthful and nodded to each other at the same time.

"Not quite as much flavor, do you think?" Ron asked.

He was right, of course.

For a brief moment, I had almost convinced myself that my wild raspberry picking days were over.

THE COWS ARE OUT!

FOURTEEN

Brigette

The frosted ferns on the milk room window blocked my view one morning. The previous night's temperature had plummeted well below zero and each barn window exhibited a frozen work of art. As I leaned forward and blew a circle in the frost to peek outside, I was reminded of a girlhood winter ritual. Before going to sleep, I lay at the foot of my bed next to the window and blew two peepholes in the frost and looked out over the lights of Caribou, listening for the sound of evening curfew — nine strikes of the Methodist Church bell.

Because I couldn't see outside, I looked around the inside of the milk room and noticed the deep grooves in the milk room door. They were made by the toenails of our Saint Bernard, Brigette. Brigette had died three years earlier.

Brigette's summer habit was to lie outside under the milk room window. In winter, she made a bed of hay in front of the cows. Pity the cow that reached for the hay near her. Her snap warned the cow that it was her hay, at least until she finished napping. When Brigette needed to get outside, she opened the

Me with some of Brigette's second litter of puppies, 1977.

two-way swinging door with her huge paw and hustled through
before it closed.

Even though it had been three years since we had to put her down, I still expected to see her come through the milk room door. And I often thought I heard her sniffs, sneezes and yawns. I even expected her giant head to push up under my hand and demand patting, and I still waited for her tail to thump against my leg. I missed her terribly.

When we started to look for a dog, a Saint Bernard seemed right for the open spaces of our farm. Our veterinarian, George, knew a family who raised Saints, so he offered to contact them for us. One fall afternoon George appeared with Brigette, a seven-week-old, short-haired female. She had perfect Saint Bernard markings — a deep auburn color with pure white feet, tail, and ruff. A narrow, white strip divided her black mask. The white strip on her head was topped with an auburn spot the size of a quarter. Even at seven weeks, she seemed to fill the back hallway.

During the next twelve years she became watchdog, cat chaser, best friend to Kyle and Travis, chum to hired help, mother of twenty-six puppies, and my devoted companion.

Dr. George checked Brigette's hips and deemed them perfect. He thought she was well bred and good looking enough to breed, if we could find the right male. He said she may come into heat before she turned one, but to skip that first heat and wait for at least one more before breeding her.

"Watch her closely," George warned us, "so that when she does come into heat, she doesn't get bred too young to a mutt."

"How will we know when she's in heat?" I asked.

"You'll know!" George laughed.

Ron assumed the task of housebreaking Brigette. The fall was cool, but he bundled up and faithfully walked her across the dooryard and beyond the driveway to a nearby field. After several weeks of this routine, she seemed to understand.

One blustery day, Ron decided it was time for Brigette to go outside by herself. He opened the door and she hurried out. After she went through the shed door, she stopped and looked around for Ron, and waited for him. After several minutes, Brigette went, turned her back, squatted and did her business in front of the steps.

After a few more weeks of Ron's faithful accompaniment, Brigette finally learned her spot and continued to use it for many years. When she was nine, a new barn was constructed right on her spot, but she would not give it up even during construction. Finally, when the doors were hung and she could no longer gain entry, she reluctantly went behind the new barn.

One day, several months after Brigette was housebroken, Ron came through the back door and asked, "Where's Brigette? She was right here in the yard with me and now she's nowhere in sight."

I looked out the kitchen window. Brigette was across the road in the orchard, three dogs chasing her. Ron called to her and Brigette looked his way, but continued to run with the pack. When Brigette saw Ron running after her, she left the pack to hide under a pine tree. Ron crawled under the tree and pulled her out. Both were panting when he returned holding her by the collar.

"Do you think she got tagged?" I asked.

"Who knows," he replied. "She must be in heat or she wouldn't have run away."

We called Dr. George to say that we thought Brigette just got bred by a traveling salesman. We took her to Dr. George's office and, to prevent conception, he immediately gave her a hormone shot. Along with our relief that we had prevented puppies on Brigette's first heat came the news that the hormone

treatment would prolong her heat. We would have to confine
her for at least a week. Unless accompanied outside by one of
the family, Brigette spent the next week in the kitchen.

As a serious watchdog, Brigette had a reputation even with
people who had never seen her. A warning — "Don't pat the
dog" — came before any greeting to visitors. She allowed patting on her terms only. Those who didn't listen and tried to pat
her anyway found their hand in her mouth. She didn't bite, but
the feeling of her teeth and saliva convinced them that the next
move was hers. She usually circled the person, sniffed shoes and
pant legs, and then either walked away or nudged her head up
under their hand after she decided they were okay.

"Try to ignore her," I suggested, but people found it
difficult to ignore one hundred sixty pounds of fur and flesh
growling at them.

Brigette guarded her territory with a vengeance. Because
her territory included the road in front of the farm, she disliked people walking by and especially disliked runners, bikers
and snowmobilers. I told walkers that if they ignored her
barks, she usually lost interest and sauntered back to the
house. I encouraged runners to slow to a walk and not talk or
shout. I warned bikers to get off their bikes and walk by on
the opposite side of the road. One boy tried to out-pedal her,
and Brigette came back to the house with the heel of his shoe
in her mouth.

One morning as I washed the milk dishes in the milk
room, I heard someone scream my name. I raced to the end of
the driveway and there in the field across the road was a runner,
jogging in place, with stick in hand. Brigette stood braced and
ready for him to advance. "Git, git!" he screamed, waving the
stick, "git away from me!"

It was Jim Reed, one of Travis's teachers. Travis will probably never pass English now, I thought.

"Just stand still and stop screaming," I shouted as I ran down the road.

"She's got me cornered!" he said.

I looked out over the forty-acre field. As I grabbed Brigette's collar, he jogged backwards away from her, never taking his eyes off her.

"I'm sorry about that," I said, "but I'm sure the stick didn't help. If you would just walk by instead of running and ignore her, I really don't think she'd bother you."

"I can't do that," he said. "It ruins my pace; and look at her — she knows that I'm terrified of her." Brigette barked and lunged forward as I restrained her by the collar.

"Jim, please call me when you plan to run by and I'd be glad to put her in the house. Then we'll all be more comfortable."

"I'll do that," he said, as he resumed his running. "I certainly will do that."

Because they could outdistance her, I had no advice for snowmobilers, but I tried to train Brigette not to cross the road where the snowmobile trail passed our farm.

At precisely two-thirty on weekday afternoons, no matter where she was, Brigette came to the front lawn, lay down and waited. At three o'clock, the school bus slowed and stopped in front of the farm. Brigette wagged her tail even before she arose and trotted across the lawn to greet Kyle, Travis, and sometimes Danny as they stepped off the bus.

When the boys played in the yard, she either joined in their games or lay nearby while they played. Brigette's favorite game was tug-of-war with a rag. She usually won because she outweighed them. During one match with Travis, Brigette lost hold of the rag and Travis fell backwards on the grass. Brigette ran to him, sniffed the rag and nuzzled his arms, trying to free the rag as he clutched it to his chest. Unable to retrieve the rag from Travis, she circled him, grabbed the hood of his sweatshirt and dragged him across the lawn.

Travis and Brigette had special communications concerning the barn cats. "Brigie," Travis whispered loudly, "get the caaaat! Go get the caaaat!" as he patted her rump and pointed to a cat. I don't think it was what he said but the way he said it. Brigette would tear after the cat. If the cat ran, the chase was on until the cat found a hiding place. Then Brigette trotted back to Travis for praise. Even if she caught the cat or the cat didn't attempt a getaway, she never harmed one. She just nuzzled it with her huge black nose and looked back at Travis for approval.

When signs of Brigette's second heat became evident, we searched for an appropriate male.

We located a long-haired Saint in Palermo. The family agreed to let Brandy come to our farm and stay as long as necessary. They assured us that Brandy was AKC registered and that the necessary papers would be provided if we allowed them pick of the litter.

When Brandy first arrived, Brigette ignored him. As the week wore on, she became interested, but he was standoffish. By the third week, we wondered if she was really in heat. The fertile time is at the very end of the heat cycle, so we gave them a few more days.

By the end of that week, Brigette grew very active and friendly toward Brandy, who by this time had completely adjusted to farm life and lazed around as though he'd been born

Travis (on the left) with Kyle and Danny and some of Brigette's puppies in the early 1970s.

on the place. Brigette leaned on him, lapped him, lay beside him, even backed up to him, but Brandy looked the other way.

"I don't think he's got it in him," I said. "All he wants to do is eat and sleep."

The next day, county FHA personnel arrived with a group of Africans to tour our farm. Brigette and Brandy greeted the visitors as they stepped from their cars. After introductions, Ron began telling them about our farm. At that moment, Brandy decided it was time and he finally began his performance. Ron looked at me expectantly and I returned a shrug. Ron continued talking, but soon realized that he had lost center stage as Brandy mounted Brigette and they moved toward the group together. Wide-eyed, some of the visitors stepped aside and began to whisper to each other.

"Do something with those dogs!" Ron said desperately.

Realizing by now that Brandy had to go wherever Brigette went, I called her away from the group and pled with her to go out on the front lawn. That didn't work, so I went behind them and gently nudged them along, and whenever Brigette looked around at Brandy, I waved my hands in that direction. Ron continued his speech as the three of us disappeared around the corner of the house. Once on the front lawn, the performance slowed passing traffic. I continued my mission and successfully directed them to the back lawn, where they remained attached. I hid in the house until all the cars left the driveway. When I went out again, I met Ron on his way from the barn.

"What did you think of that scene?" he asked.

"I was a bit embarrassed," I replied.

"Embarrassed? I was mortified," he said. "I wanted to show the Africans our Holstein cows, not Saint Bernards mating."

"It may turn out to be the highlight of their trip, who knows?" I said.

Just then Brigette rounded the corner of the house in a trot, wiggling her rear end and woofing her delight each time she pranced by us.

"Looks as though she enjoyed the encounter," I said.

"I'm glad she did," Ron said, "because I sure didn't."

The next day Brandy's owners picked him up, and Brigette settled down for an eight-week gestation period. When she got close to her due date, we prepared a nest of hay for her in an empty horse stall. She gave birth to thirteen puppies, ten of which survived.

Raising puppies is high on my list of life's most enjoyable times. Five puppies were short-haired and five were long-haired. Their personalities emerged as soon as they opened their eyes

My pal Brigette and me.

and started to waddle around. The dominant one pushed its way to the teat, while the runt fell away, got up and tried again. The first pups to bark became aggressive, the shy pups sat back and watched, and the friendly ones ran to us for fondling.

The puppies grew quickly, but because Brandy's owners could not produce the proper papers, their value was not as great as we had hoped. Instead of $100 each, we knew we would be lucky to get $25.

We knew it was time to start selling the puppies when they were eating ten pounds of dog food a day. Tears were shed, but eventually all the pups went to farms or rural homes where they probably didn't have to be tied up. The runt of the litter went to farmer friends in New York.

I think because I fed her and meals were very important to her, Brigette liked me best. Wherever I went, she was beside me. If I raked hay, she lumbered along beside the tractor, tongue hanging from the side of her mouth, dripping perspiration. If I rode Jud, she followed us. When I fed the calves, she made every trip to and from the milk room and waited, not always patiently, to lick clean the milk left in the bottom of the pails.

I welcomed Brigette's companionship everywhere except in the garden. Try as I might, I couldn't convince her to stay on the edge while I worked in the garden. She sat on the edge at my command until my back was turned. Then she got up and silently came up behind me and sat down, usually on the newly sprouted peas or beans. She liked to browse in the garden even when I wasn't there. What destruction those huge paws could do to a row of lettuce or corn!

During her last two years, Brigette became deaf and suffered from arthritis in her shoulders. With help and advice from Dr. George, Brigette lived to be twelve years old — two, perhaps, three years older than an average Saint.

In her final days, Brigette's health steadily declined. Finally, after a week when she couldn't even get up, I called George and asked him to come out. Although Brigette and George were the best of friends, she usually objected to his professional attention. But on this day she seemed resigned, even welcomed his presence. After all, he was the one who had brought her into our lives. Travis and I held and patted her. As George prepared to administer the fatal needle, Brigette barked at a passerby and struggled to get up to perform her watch duty one last time.

We buried her next to the garden.

FIFTEEN

Stuck in a Snowbank

During the period when both Ella and Vicki were part of our milking herd, we kept thirty-six cows tied up in the barn. After going outside for daily exercise, each cow returned to an assigned stall. Each cow had a different stall every year because cows spent their dry period in another barn, resting for two months before calving and rejoining the milking string. By the time the cow returned to the milking herd, her stall was being used by another cow that had calved before her.

An older cow usually learned to identify her new stall in two or three days. It might take a young first-calf heifer up to two months. But Ella, our most nervous cow, had real difficulty learning her new stall. Her herd mate, Vicki, was even worse. To make matters more difficult, Vicki's stall was located at the end of the barn, meaning she had to pass by all the others, including Ella's, to reach it. Every day when Vicki entered the barn, no matter how many people guided her, she blindly entered practically every stall along the way to hers. As each cow followed and discovered that Vicki or the cow she had displaced occupied her stall, a ripple effect occurred — otherwise known as chaos.

One morning, with that chaos in full swing, Ron slammed the overhead barn door down to keep some cows out while we sorted the ones already inside. He urged Vicki toward her place at the end of the barn.

After chasing her in and out of numerous stalls, I said, "Vicki is so dumb, let's put her near the door so she won't have as many stalls to try out before she gets to hers. Remember what Leland always told us: 'It's a matter of who outwits who.' "

"And you remember that Dr. George says cows are smarter than horses," Ron retorted.

"Smart is not the right word for cows," I replied. "I think some cows may be less dumb than others, but Vicki is the dumbest heifer I've ever seen."

"She'll learn her stall," Ron said with determination. "It may take a little longer, but she'll learn."

To Ron, putting Vicki in a different stall close to the door meant giving Vicki her way, and not outwitting her. And Ron was determined to have *his* way. So, Ron didn't change Vicki's stall, and she tested his wits every morning.

One February morning, while the cows explored the snowy barnyard, we cleaned the inside of the barn. After we apportioned the grain and scraped and bedded the stalls, Ron opened the door to let the cows back in. Vicki ran in and jumped right into Ella's stall. Ella, who was directly behind her, stopped by her stall and looked to one side, then to the other.

"Wait a second, Ella," I heard Ron say calmly. "Take it easy. I'll get Vicki out of your stall."

Of all the stalls she could have picked, I thought, it would have to be Ella's. As Ron stepped into the stall to turn Vicki, Ella spun around and raced back outside. Ron shut the door until we successfully herded Vicki to her stall, secured her neck chain, and rearranged several other cows.

"Where's Ella?" I asked, after all the other cows had come into the barn and were chained up.

"She's still out back of the barn. Probably too nervous to come in now," Ron said. "I'll go get her."

The fence around the barnyard had drifted in, and one side was completely covered by a bank of plowed snow. I watched out the window as Ron approached Ella.

"Go on, Ella, the door is that way," Ron said, pointing in the direction of the barn door. Brigette trotted back and forth, barking her directions, too. Ella stiffened and plunged her front legs into the snow bank.

"I said, *that* way," Ron commanded. He climbed the bank to get in front of Ella, which frightened her even more. She dug in with her rear legs. Brigette stood watching from the top of the snowbank as Ella clambered over it and stood belly-deep in the crusted snow.

Standing hip-deep in the snow in front of her, Ron shouted, "Turn around, you hammerhead, get around there!" Ella's wild eyes stared first at the human who roared and waved his arms and then at the canine who barked and flopped her ears. Ella lunged forward, dragging her udder through the cold snow.

"Bring out a halter," Ron yelled.

Seeing me hurry through the barnyard with a halter distressed Ella even more. She leapt forward again. Ron secured the halter and tried to pull her head around to the path that she had broken through the snow. In spite of Ron's efforts, Ella would not budge.

"She's stuck," Ron said. "Bring out a shovel."

Ron began shoveling through the bank toward Ella's rear. The more he shoveled, the more she lunged forward, blowing huge puffs of steam from her nostrils. Then she began to shiver.

"She's going to freeze her bag if we don't get her out soon," Ron panted, sweat streaming down his temples.

Ron continued shoveling until he reached her tail end. "You're as dumb as Vicki," he said, wading through the snow to her head. Then he pulled on her halter to turn her around. The harder he pulled on the halter, the harder she resisted. She then dodged his attempts to tap her head with the shovel, turned away, and rested her head on the snow.

"I guess I'll have to shovel a path in front of her," Ron said desperately. "We can't leave her here much longer or she won't have any teats left."

As Ron cleared a circular path in front of her, I nudged Ella along from behind, and Brigette barked and bounded through the snow beside her. Near exhaustion, Ella finally conceded and stumbled along behind Ron as he broke through the snowbank into the barnyard.

She staggered and limped toward the door, entered the barn, and found her stall. Steam rolled off her wet body and she trod nervously as Ron checked the scratches on her udder. Luckily, all four teats were still intact.

"If Ella wasn't such a good producer, I'd take her to the butcher!" Ron said, although, I knew he didn't mean it.

But from that time on, Ella stayed behind until all the other cows entered the barn and only one stall remained empty — hers. And we did not change Vicki's stall on her next lactation.

SIXTEEN

Death of a Silky

We kept an old chicken coop in the backyard. Uncle Albert told us that it was once shared by Minnie and Mina, elderly twin sisters who had lived in our house many years ago. The coop was partitioned down the middle. Minnie kept her flock of laying hens on one side, and Mina kept hers on the other. Albert said they separated their flocks to see whose hens laid the most eggs.

I used one side of the old coop to house two pigs, and I used the other side to keep a few laying hens. I shoveled fresh sawdust into that side and put up some nests, a feed trough, and a waterer.

After my hens had settled into their new home, they began producing their first pullet eggs. It was a treat to collect the fresh eggs and see how firmly they stood in the frying pan; yolks didn't break and run all over the pan like store-bought eggs. And the taste of a store-bought egg can't compare to that of a freshly laid one.

At that time Dr. George was fresh out of school and eager for experience. He kept a log on my flock, observing them at least once a week when he came to buy eggs or check our herd. If one ailed, he advised or performed treatment. If one died, he did an autopsy to determine cause of death. One day, he showed up with a chicken crate in the back of his car.

"I'm interested in exotic fowl," George said, "so I ordered a couple of Japanese Silky Bantam roosters. They aren't getting along all that well, so I thought you might keep one for me on loan. I'll take him back if he's any problem."

I peeked into the backseat of his car. The Silky was hunched against the corner of the crate, obviously not happy with his transport.

"He's not very big," I remarked. "Can he hold his own?"

"Oh, sure, and he'll keep the hens active, stir them around so they eat and drink more. I'll bet they'll lay more."

Reluctantly, I accepted his dubious loan of a black, fluffy, cocky little banty. When George tossed the Silky into the coop, the hens scattered, wings flapping, feathers flying. He slowly strutted around, twitching his head from side to side, checking out his new quarters. As he circled the perimeter, the hens scurried into a bunch and crouched under the roost, clucking all sorts of strange greetings. When he spied the grain trough, he pecked, stealing glances at the hens in between bites. One by one the curious hens cautiously approached the banty, stepping tentatively in a wide circle. If they came closer than he liked, he shook his comb and they scattered.

"Think they like him?" I asked.

"They're interested," George replied, "and at least they're not attacking him, like heifers do a bull when first turned into the pasture with them."

After several days, the Silky ruled the roost. When he stepped up to the grain trough, the hens parted to make room for him. When he approached them from the rear, they squatted, arched their wings, bowed their heads, and braced their feet, ready for his service — which he provided regularly. At first he avoided me and ran under the roost while I fed grain and changed the water. Each day he became a little braver, coming just a bit closer to me while I collected eggs. Then, one day, he rushed over to the door when he saw me approach the coop. At first I thought he was trying to escape. Then I realized that he resented my presence and wanted to keep me out and away from his flock. I shooed him aside and proceeded to collect eggs.

I eyed him warily while I bent to pick eggs from the nests. He followed me, but backed away when I turned to look at him. As soon as I turned my back, though, he was at my heels.

"That Silky of yours is getting quite brave," I told George. "I can usually get rid of him with a glare, but yesterday I had to stamp my foot at him because he didn't back off."

"He doesn't want you invading his domain," George said. "Watch him, because he has sharp spurs on his legs and he may try to use them."

After George's warning, I was careful not to take my eyes off the banty when I was in the coop. One day when I reached under a hen to check for eggs, she squawked her objections. The noise brought the banty to my heels. When I lifted my foot to shoo him away, he flapped his wings, attacked me and dug his spurs into the calf of my leg, pecking on my shin at the same time. I dropped my basket of eggs.

"Get off me!" I screamed, shaking my leg. "Get away from me!" He dismounted, ran to the corner of the coop, and hid behind the hens who were frightened into a collective heap. I picked up my basket of cracked eggs and hurried out. The next day I took a broom into the coop with me. The banty circled me. When I shook the broom at him, he flew at it just like he attacked my leg, so I flung it at him and knocked him against the nests. This time, he didn't seek refuge behind his flock, but retreated to a corner by himself and crouched.

One morning I asked Travis, eight years old at the time, to collect eggs for breakfast. "But watch the banty," I said. "I take the broom in with me and he doesn't come near."

When Travis came through the shed door, I knew by his clamped jaw and pursed lips that he and the banty had tangled.

"What happened?" I asked.

"He tried to jump on my leg, that jerk, but I kicked him. Then he kept coming back again and again, so I taught him a lesson."

"Did you hit him with the broom?" I asked.

"No."

"What did you do?"

"Come see."

I followed Travis back to the chicken coop and looked inside. "Where is he? I don't see him," I said.

"He's over there hiding under the nests," he scowled.

From the outside of the wire-covered door, we stooped to find the banty peeking nervously from under the nests.

"He looks wet," I said.

"He is," Travis said.

"How did he get wet?"

"I sprayed him with the garden hose."

For several days the banty hid under the nests whenever I was in the coop.

"Has the banty bothered you lately, Mom?" Travis asked later that week.

"No," I said, "but he's not his usual lively self. He looks droopy and hides under the nests when I go into the coop. I haven't seen him eat or drink or even stir the hens."

The Silky died several days later.

I knew that he was feeling poorly, but I didn't think he was close to death. I dreaded telling George, but he was at the farm the next day, so I broke the news.

"Your Japanese Silky has expired," I said as gently as I could.

"That's hard to believe," George said. "He was so young and frisky. Let me look at him."

I left him to his autopsy.

After George had completed the task, he shook his head. "This is peculiar," he said, "but I think that Silky died of pneumonia."

"Hmmmm," was all I could say.

THE COWS ARE OUT!

SEVENTEEN

Pickin' Rocks: A Recipe for Life

Ingredients:
Old friends and kids
Summer breeze
Hard work
Lunch
Sunshine

Directions:
Mix together old friends and kids at least once a year. Add summer breeze and hard work. Blend carefully. Top with lunch once a day and bake in sunshine for one week. Watch carefully for renewal of body and spirit.

"How many sandwiches should I make for you, Bob?" I asked our visiting friend as I packed a picnic lunch in preparation for the day's work on Beaver Hill.

"Oh, I don't eat lunch," Bob replied.

"Nothing at all?" I queried.

"No, thanks," he said. "I'm not in the habit of eating any lunch because I don't do anything to work up an appetite. Those blueberry pancakes you made this morning will hold me until suppertime."

"Bob, pickin' rocks is different than sitting at a desk," I said. "I'll guarantee you'll be hungry by noon."

"No," Bob said. "I eat breakfast and a big supper at home and that suits me fine."

"Okay," I said, but I knew he'd never picked rocks before and didn't really know what hard work it was. Bob Bloch and Ron had been in the Marine Corps together, and since he and his wife had children the same ages as our boys, Sue and I had swapped babysitting and supported each other while our husbands were away on military cruises. We had grown close over the years. Almost every summer, they visited us for a week.

Still, our ways of life could not have been more opposite. After Bob's military discharge, he chose a career with IBM and worked in Philadelphia.

During this visit, Bob and his son Robbie were helping us on our Beaver Hill land, which was six miles from the farm. When we lost the use of one hundred acres of rented land in 1978, we borrowed more money to purchase the Beaver Hill property. Our part of The Hill consisted of fifty-five acres of tillage and twenty-three acres of woods.

Once there had been several small farms on the property and traces were still visible. An old barn remained on one section and maple trees surrounded the rock foundation where the house once stood. A dug well and apple trees marked the location of another long-abandoned small farm. A pile of old boards was all that remained on the premises of still another farm, but wild rose bushes and columbine lingered in memory of the

Picking rocks on Beaver Hill in Freedom, 1985. Ron is driving the Massey-Ferguson 1105 while Scott Anderson and I pick up missed rocks.

farmers who had worked there. Back then, thirty or forty acres supported their needs, but now our farm required two hundred and thirty acres to support what had become a fifty-cow herd plus offspring.

Our newest fields had been fallow for several years and now needed to be plowed and reworked so we could plant alfalfa.

This being Maine, many rocks were brought to the surface by the plow. We had already removed large washing machine-sized rocks with crowbars and lots of grunting. We had scooped them up with the tractor and front-end loader and dumped them at the edge of the field, adding to the rock walls started by the farmers of past generations. Meanwhile, football-sized rocks were moved into rows by a rock rake, a huge corkscrew-shaped roller pulled over the ground by a tractor. A mechanical rock picker, also pulled by a tractor, then picked up the rows of rocks. It scooped both the rocks and soil and carried them up onto metal lags or rods. The soil fell through the spaces and back to the ground while the lags carried the rocks into a bucket on the back of the rock picker. The full bucket of rocks was either dumped into a truck and hauled to the edge of the field, or the rock picker itself was backed up to the edge of the field and its contents dumped onto the rock wall.

After several weeks of removing rocks, we decided that the glacier that had once passed over North America must have stopped and melted on Beaver Hill, leaving all the rocks it had accumulated throughout its journey.

"This is a large day," Ron remarked when we arrived on Beaver Hill, a statement he often made on a perfect summer day.

Kyle drove the rock picker as Bob, Robbie, Travis, Ron, and I followed along, picking up and tossing into the bucket any rocks that the rock picker had missed or that had been pushed aside by the scoop. Bend, pick, toss; bend, pick, toss.

The smell of the earth as we picked rocks made me homesick for Aroostook County where I spent many fall days as a young girl picking potatoes. As we walked along on the soft, brown cushion, I started to daydream.

What a special place to just *be*, I thought. I belong here on The Hill, in this wonderfully isolated space, with the breeze blowing the clutter from my head, the sun warming my shoulders, renewing my spirit, and expanding my dreams until they seemed real. With every rock I touched, I felt a bond to this small parcel of earth, a bond so strong it seemed as though I had worked this land before in another time, another life. This is good earth, I thought, that will reward us with the best crop of alfalfa. I didn't mind at all that the earth got into my shoes, crusted around my fingernails, coated my arms and hands, and blew into my hair.

At lunchtime we welcomed shade and sat under the trees that lined the rock walls along the edges of the field. I poured iced tea and passed out sandwiches to everyone except Bob.

"Aren't you hungry after picking rocks all morning?" I asked.

"A little," Bob admitted.

"I'll share my sandwich with you," I said, as I unwrapped mine.

"No, thanks, Trudy, I'm fine, really. This iced tea hits the spot, though."

"How about a carrot stick from my garden?" I asked, as I passed the plastic bag full of sliced carrots.

"I think I could eat some of those if you have plenty," Bob replied. Then we sat eating quietly, viewing the distant hills and mountains.

"You're so quiet, Bob," Ron said after lunch, as he lay back on the grass and folded his hands behind his head.

"I'm making the transition between my work and here," Bob said. "I get depressed with my job at IBM. Sometimes it's so boring that I dread going to work in the morning. You seem to look forward to your day's work. Do you know how lucky you are?"

"I think I do, Bob," said Ron. "I've always known that I wanted to farm and I've never wavered from that. I can truly say that I enjoy what I do."

He studied Bob for a moment. "Why not do something else if you're not happy with your work?"

"I've worked almost twenty years for IBM," Bob said. "I'm too young to retire, and if I quit now, I'd lose my pension. Besides, they're a good company to work for. I get five weeks of vacation every year, they pay for moving my family whenever I relocate, and I make an excellent salary. Sometimes I'm unhappy with the job, but I can't leave the company now. I guess I'll have to stick it out."

That night, we sat down to a meal that had been entirely farm-grown — venison chops from a spike horn deer that Travis had shot last fall; potatoes, corn, cucumbers and tomatoes from our garden; and raspberry pie from raspberries I had picked along the rock wall. And, of course, there was milk from our cows. We didn't always have enough money to pay the bills, but we always ate well.

Bob remarked, "I think I used some muscles today that I've never used before." His nose was sunburned and his eyes were bloodshot. "Are we pickin' rocks again tomorrow?"

"You bet," Ron said with a smile.

"Then I'll be going to bed early tonight," Bob said, "that is, after I take a shower. Won't it feel good to get clean again."

"How many sandwiches should I make for you today?" I asked Bob, as I packed a picnic lunch the following morning.

"I think I could eat half a sandwich today," Bob replied. "I must admit that I was a bit hungry by lunchtime yesterday."

The second day proved to be as beautiful as the first, and the view of the dark green woods, blending with layers of purple and blue hills nestled in front of the hazy White Mountains, was splendid.

"Isn't this a beautiful place!" I remarked.

"Sure is," Bob replied. "What mountains can we see from here?"

"The Bigelow Chain is over there," I said, as I pointed to the west, "and beyond them, the White Mountains of New Hampshire. To the north is Mount Katahdin, Maine's highest."

"Do you ever think of building a house up here?" he asked.

"Yes," I said. "Every day."

We ate lunch after we had finished the first field and before we moved to the second. I poured lemonade for everyone and passed out sandwiches. Bob seemed anxious for lunch and ate his half sandwich quickly, then nibbled on carrots.

"Dad, I have two sandwiches," Robbie said. "I'll share another half of a sandwich with you."

"I'll split a half with you, Robbie, and that's it for me today. I'll be putting on weight, first thing I know."

After lunch, Ron lay back under the trees, folded his muscular arms across his chest and within a minute after he closed his eyes, he breathed deeply.

"He's asleep!" said Bob. "How can he go to sleep so fast?"

"Catnaps are his salvation," I replied. "He works hard and rarely gets more than five or six hours of sleep at night, so a five- or ten-minute catnap rejuvenates him for another few hours. The best thing is that he always wakes in a good mood, raring to go."

"Let's get started on the next field," Ron said as he stood up and stretched.

Ron took a turn operating the rock picker while the three boys, Bob, and I trailed behind. Bend, pick, toss; bend, pick, toss.

While we were picking we spotted an eagle circling overhead. The wondrous bird, with its eight-foot wing span, seemed to watch us, too, as it glided across the pale blue sky, looking down upon the smooth brown carpet where six of us stood, shading our eyes with hands to our foreheads, as though we were saluting.

"I wonder if there's a nest nearby," Travis said, when the eagle had drifted lower and finally disappeared over Freedom Pond.

"Makes the whole day worthwhile after seeing that beautiful creature," I said.

Bob agreed.

The next morning Bob looked over my shoulder and asked what I was packing for lunch.

"Fluffer-nutters," I said. "How many for you?"

"Today I could eat one and a half, I think. Are the cookies for lunch, too?"

"Yes, chocolate-chip. Lemonade and carrot sticks, too."

"Sounds good to me," Bob said, as he helped gather the lunch together.

"I thought you were the one who didn't eat lunch?" I asked with a chuckle.

"Well, I do work up an appetite pickin' rocks, and I don't think I'm gaining weight, either."

During the days we spent on The Hill that week, Bob joked and laughed, gradually becoming his old self, the one we had known years before when he and Ron had been lieutenants together.

"Maybe I can get transferred to Maine," Bob said one afternoon.

"Would IBM have a position in Maine?" Ron asked.

"Portland is a possibility," Bob replied. "If I could get away from Philadelphia, it might make the job easier to take. I think I'll try for a transfer when I get home."

He looked serious for a moment and then broke into a smile. "Ron, do you believe that I actually like pickin' rocks?"

As I prepared lunch for our last day of pickin' rocks on The Hill, I decided not to ask Bob how many sandwiches he wanted. He had a wide smile when he came through the back door after helping with the morning barn chores. "Two sandwiches for me today, please."

EIGHTEEN

Life and Death in the Field

Mowing hay was one of my favorite farm jobs. But along with its pleasures, such as fragrant breezes and ever-changing scenery, came occasional mini-disasters — the killing of small animals by my tractor. Mice, snakes, birds, and butterflies, evicted from their homes when we plowed and planted, were evicted again when I mowed. Most creatures were frightened away by the noise of the machines, but those who weren't often became an easy lunch for gulls and crows.

One day, I was mowing a newly seeded hay field on Beaver Hill. Because it was a large piece, I divided my job into three sections. I watched the lush alfalfa, timothy, and sweet-smelling clover fall into neat rows behind the new mower that seemed to float over the terrain. Indian paintbrush and purple vetch bloomed along the ditch of the bordering dirt road, fluttering poplar leaves framed the field, and a cloudless view of the western mountains set the stage for the day. After finishing the first, I began mowing the middle section of the field.

Thud!

Oh, no.

I stopped the tractor and sat for a few moments looking back at the windrow of hay. I knew I had to investigate, so I stepped down and hesitantly approached the heap of tan and white fur. As I drew closer, I could see the vivid spots of a fawn. I stood frozen, staring at the innocent dead baby whose mother had probably taught her to stay in her hiding place — the field we shared. She was taught how to avoid natural enemies, not machines.

My anguished sighs did nothing to lighten the lead in my stomach. I turned toward the Bennett's farmhouse and noticed Steve and his son, Matt, playing basketball in the yard. I walked over to them and asked, "Have you seen any deer in your field this year?"

"Yes, we've seen as many as eight or nine at a time in the lower field near the woods," Steve replied, "but I haven't seen any lately."

They came out last night, I thought, to eat the sweet clover and tender alfalfa leaves that we'd planted. "Well," I said, "I just ran over a fawn."

"Oh, no," Steve replied as he set the basketball down and walked in the direction of the casualty.

"I never saw the fawn," I said despondently.

"You wouldn't expect one to be in the middle of a field," he assured me.

"It's so small," I said. "Maybe it's a twin and there's another one hiding around here." Matt and I tramped and searched through the tall hay in the surrounding area for another one, while Steve disposed of the dead fawn.

When Steve returned from the woods, I said, "Thanks, I could have taken care of that myself, but I guess I just needed to tell someone."

That's me chopping haylage on Beaver Hill in the mid-1980s.

"The fawn was small," Steve said. "I wouldn't be surprised if there were another one."

After a rest under the trees, I returned to mowing. I stood up on the tractor as I drove and watched more closely, trying hard to notice paths in the hay or flattened spots in front of the mower. If there were twins, I thought, they probably bedded together. I relaxed a bit after I finished the middle section of the field and no other fawn had appeared. Still keeping a watchful eye, I continued mowing the last section near the woods.

After five or six times around, I suddenly saw a quick movement behind me. Then, out of its hiding place sprung the other fawn. She was all but in flight as she skimmed the top of

121

the hay on young, slender legs seemingly no bigger around than my little finger. Her spots were a blur as she raced by the mower. Before I could draw a breath, she disappeared into the woods. I stopped, rubbed the goose bumps on my arms, and laughed with relief.

What had caused her to leave her hiding place? Did my machine frighten her? Did her mother send a signal? Whatever the reason, I was thankful.

NINETEEN

On Call Round-the-Clock

If forced to explain in simple terms how all-consuming and demanding running a farm is, I might compare it to caring for a newborn baby — one that never grows up and must be watched round-the-clock, three hundred sixty-five days a year. The days are long, the nights are short, and the work is never done.

For us, some chores came on a steady, reliable, even if never-ending, schedule. For example, the cows needed to be milked every twelve hours, regardless. Milking the cows and its required schedule established the base rhythm of farm life.

Other duties adhered to no schedule and could occur at any time — calvings, for example. Frequent births on a farm require you to always be on call. Ninety percent of the time, a cow gives birth just fine without human help. Still, you never know when you'll be needed to assist with a breech birth, multiple births, or a twisted uterus. We preferred to be present for all births — just in case. After all, this was our livelihood.

On her second visit to our farm in the early 1980s, Kyle's college girlfriend and future wife, Karen, was thrilled that she would get to see a live birth. Karen had been raised in New York, and had never actually seen a cow up close until she came to visit Craneland Farm for the first time. Now, she wanted to watch a birth. As she arrived, the grand event was due at any moment.

"The feet are out. Kyle, are you going to deliver this one?" I asked.

"If you get a pail of water and the chain, I'll put some fresh bedding in her pen," Kyle said. Karen watched anxiously from the side of the calving pen as Kyle and I washed our hands in iodine solution and dunked the chain and handles into the pail. I held the feet of the calf as he looped the ends of the chain around each ankle.

"Big feet," I said. "Must be a bull." Then I prayed that it would be a heifer.

"She's not helping much, not straining at all now," Kyle said. "Let's put the handles on the chain and tug a little, then maybe she'll push if she feels our help."

"It's her first time," I told Karen. "She doesn't know what this is all about."

As the nose appeared it, too, looked large, and the opening through which it must pass, small.

"Better run and get Dad," Kyle said to Karen. "He's out in the shop."

Karen seemed to welcome an errand and, without a word, ran out the door.

"We need someone stronger than I am," I said as Ron came to the pen. "Nanny's not helping."

Ron vaulted over the side of the pen and rolled up his sleeves. "Big feet," he said, also washing his hands in the iodine solution. "Karen, pass me some hay to put under the calf's head as it comes out. Trudy, ease the head through the vulva with your hands."

The calf's tongue was blue and dangled.

"This is taking too long," I said. "The calf isn't showing any signs of life."

"We're doing the best we can," Ron said as he and Kyle pulled each time Nanny pushed with her contractions.

"How are you doing?" Kyle asked, looking up at Karen.

"A little queasy," she said, patting her belly.

Finally, the calf's head popped through the opening, but the eyes were motionless.

"It's a red-and-white calf," Kyle said. "This is our first one."

After Nanny strained several more times, the shoulders followed. She gave one last heave and the calf slid out. Ron tickled its nostrils with his fingers and touched the eyes. No response. He slapped its side to force a breath. Still no response. He felt for a heartbeat, but there was none.

"Dead," he said. "Must have been dead before we started."

He looked at Karen's pained expression. "Sorry, Karen," he said. "Not so good for your first one."

On a later visit, Karen watched Echo give birth for the first time — to a heifer. This time, it was a more joyous occasion.

After giving birth, Echo sniffed her newborn while the baby tried to hold up its heavy head. Then Echo began licking her calf vigorously.

"That's a sign of a good milk cow," Ron said, "when she owns her calf and cleans her up right away." The baby shook her head and snorted the excess fluids from her nose. She folded her front legs underneath her and lunged forward with her first attempt at standing. Then she did a somersault that covered her with sawdust again. The setback didn't bother Echo. She started all over, licking the sawdust off her baby again and glancing up at her audience occasionally. She seemed proud. Each time the calf tried to stand, she gained strength. Eventually, her rear legs stayed under her for a few moments while she knelt on her front legs. Echo continued licking her baby, pushing her off balance again.

"It's amazing, isn't it," Karen said, "the birth and how fast the calf does everything?"

As the minutes passed, the calf's fur became drier and more fluffy and the sawdust no longer stuck to her when she fell. Finally, she struggled to all four feet and stood swaying back and forth.

Her first few steps were a balancing act, but with every unsteady step, strength surged into her body. The newborn calf stepped deliberately toward her mother's udder and began to nuzzle for her first meal.

"She's trying to nurse," I said. "That didn't take long, about a half hour."

Karen's right, I thought, it *is* amazing — and every time I saw it, it still amazed me, even after twenty years.

Another calving required night work — sort of. A heifer named Glorious was carrying her first calf and began showing signs of early delivery — restlessness, treading back and forth in her stall, and getting up and down for no apparent reason. Even though she was not due to calve for ten days, Ron and I agreed that in addition to daytime checks, we should look in on her every two hours during the night. We were especially concerned because even though our veterinarian, George Holmes, owned Glorious, she had been put in our care. We knew that George was particularly fond of Glorious and considered her one of his most valuable animals.

That evening, Ron and I took turns checking. He started with the first shift at eleven o'clock. When the alarm sounded, I nudged him awake. He slipped into his work shoes and headed out to the barn. Several minutes later he returned to report, "Glorious is happy as can be. She's lying down chewing her cud."

He reset the alarm for one o'clock, plunked back into bed, and presto — he was sound asleep.

At one o'clock the alarm jolted me from a deep sleep. I arose, grudgingly, and descended the stairs. I pulled a sweatshirt over my nightgown, stepped into my Tingley boots, and trudged to the barn. There was Glorious, stretched out in her freshly bedded maternity pen. She looked sleepily at me and sighed deeply. I returned to the bed — Ron hadn't moved an inch — and reset the alarm for three-thirty. As I lay waiting to doze off, Ron stirred and mumbled something in his sleep.

"What did you say?" I asked.

"Give it to her," he answered.

Hmm, I pondered, give it to her. Should I pursue this further? Who was she and what did Ron want her to have?

"What do you want to give her?"

"Give Dora that load of haylage."

"What load of haylage?" I pressed.

"I chopped Dora a special load of haylage," he continued. "Give it to her."

"The whole load?"

"Would you just give it to her?" he responded irritably.

"Okay, I will. I'll do it," I said.

Wow, I thought, my husband talks about cows in his sleep. He really does farm twenty-four hours a day.

I fell back asleep knowing that Ron would hear the alarm at three-thirty because that was his normal time to get up and begin the morning milking.

The next night, we decided that one check at midnight would be sufficient until Glorious showed more pronounced signs of calving. After a week of alternating nights, we resumed two-hour checks because, according to the calendar, Glorious was due in two days. For another week we made our nighttime treks to and from the barn every two hours.

After two weeks of this I was exhausted, and Ron was growing impatient with Glorious.

Finally, of course, four days after her due date, Glorious delivered a huge bull calf — with no trouble — one afternoon in broad daylight.

TWENTY

Farm Girl

When I awoke at 3:45 A.M., Ron was already in the barn. My feet reached for the electric heating pad that had warmed my aching legs and frigid feet during the night. I usually warmed them on Ron, but he, too, had been cold when we went to bed. My head reeled and chills crept up my spine and enveloped my body. A wave of nausea passed over me. In a little over an hour, I would have to get up. I'll never make it in this condition, I thought. Shivering, I went to the medicine cabinet and swallowed two aspirin, threw another blanket over the bed and crawled back into the warm spot.

The alarm went off at five o'clock. My body still yearned to stay in bed, but my spirit urged me to get up and feed the calves. I had to work this off, because — well, I just had to. Both boys were away at college and there was no one else to do it. If I stayed in bed, it would take Ron and Kay two hours longer to do chores. I rolled to the edge of the bed, sat up and held my head in my hands for a few moments. I gathered my barn clothes and went downstairs where it was warmer to get dressed. Once outside, the cold air refreshed my face. On the way to the barn, I took a deep breath. The cold air tasted good, too. Sure, I could make it through one morning of chores feeling lousy.

Through the milk room window, I saw the tracks in last night's snow made by Kay's car when she arrived at ten minutes of five in the morning. Thank goodness for Kay Raven — never late for work and rarely sick.

Even now, after all these years, I could still picture Kay sitting in the fourth seat of the row near the door of my third-grade classroom. She had wavy, blond hair and sparkling blue eyes. She was a well-behaved and serious student. After her year in my classroom, I saw her only occasionally, perhaps at the corner store or passing in a car. Then, when she was a senior in high school, she came to the farm looking for a job.

"Do you have a job for me?" she asked Ron.

She was in the Cooperative Education program at school. She wanted to go to school in the morning and work in the afternoon at a job that she might be able to continue after graduation.

"I want to work on a dairy farm, but no one will hire me because I'm a girl," she said.

"Really?" Ron raised his eyebrows. "Where have you looked for a job?"

"All over, every dairy farm," Kay said with a sigh. "They say they don't need anyone, but I know it's because I'm a girl."

"Right now I have all the help I need," Ron replied.

"That's what they all say." Kay looked down and kicked at the ground. "Is it because I'm a girl?"

"No, not at all," Ron said. "If I needed help, I'd give you a chance. I already have Darrell, who comes in every afternoon to do barn chores, and Randall, who milks part time to give me a break. Besides my family, they're all the extra help I can afford."

Kay worked afternoons on her family's poultry farm, but every few months she stopped by to see if we had a job opening. Each time Ron told her that Darrell and Randall still worked for us.

One fall afternoon, after Kay had graduated from high school, she drove into the yard and stopped by the bulkhead where we were throwing wood into the cellar.

"Do you have a job for me today?"

"You really know how to put a guy on the spot, don't you?" Ron replied.

"Would you just give me a chance?" she asked. "I'll do anything. I'll shovel shit; I'll do whatever you tell me to do. I'm pretty strong, too."

"As a matter of fact," he said, "hunting season starts tomorrow and Randall and Darrell both asked for time off to go hunting. I told them they could have a few days off, so if you'll be here at six o'clock tomorrow morning, I'll give you a try."

"I'll be here!" Kay shouted and ran to her car.

She worked for us for the next nine years.

Kay was energetic, punctual, thorough, fun to work with and never idle. She looked ahead, saw what needed to be done, and did it without fanfare. She performed all of the routine barn chores — feeding the calves, cleaning out the barn and feeding the cows.

After several months, Ron asked Kay if she would like to learn to milk. Randall had asked for a few weeks off to visit relatives out west. He could show her the milking routine before he left. Kay agreed, and she became the best milker we ever had, even better than family.

After three years, Kay became interested in Jersey cows and bought a Jersey heifer to raise. (Jersey cows are a smaller breed and are usually a soft brown color. They produce less milk than larger, black-and-white Holsteins, but their milk contains more butterfat.)

She asked Ron if she could keep her cow, Bambi, with our herd, but Ron turned her down. Jerseys are smaller than Holsteins and he was afraid Bambi would get pushed around too much. Plus, Ron was a Holstein man. He told Kay about a Jersey farmer in Unity who would keep her cow. Bambi went to Unity to live, but Kay didn't lose her enthusiasm for Jerseys.

"I've been thinking that I'd like to work on a Jersey farm," she said to me one afternoon when she came to work. My heart sank, but I tried to act nonchalant.

She told me she'd met a family in Waldo who milked about a hundred Jerseys. The daughter did the milking and Kay thought it would be fun to milk with another woman. She could work more hours there and make more money.

"Are you telling me that you want to get done here?" I asked.

"Well, I want to give you a fair notice, but, yes, I would like to try working somewhere else."

"If that's what you want, you have to do it," I said sadly.

That fall Randall gave us his two-weeks notice before going to work with his father in construction. At about the same time, Kay reappeared.

"I was wondering if I could have my old job back," she said. "Randall told me he was leaving and I could get more hours without him here. Besides, I think I like Holsteins better than Jerseys. You know, I couldn't tell one Jersey from another. We milked two strings of them and we kept some cows in the barn if they had to be bred or needed treatments, and after we brought the second string in, I couldn't tell which ones I had or hadn't milked."

"The job is yours, Kay; we haven't even had a chance to look for someone to replace you," Ron said with a smile.

Several years later, Kay announced that she planned to
attend a Bible college in New York. We were glad that she had
decided to further her education, but we were sorry that it was
while Kyle was also away at college. In the early 1980s, we had
decided to auction off part of our milking herd to raise enough
money to pay off some existing debt. With the decreased herd
size, we also decided to do the work ourselves, with only Travis
and Darrell's help.

Kay's first letter from college was filled with news of her new
activities, piano lessons, and all the studying she was doing. In
the second letter she sounded less content. Panty hose and skirts
were required dress, and taking a walk on Sunday afternoon
strongly suggested — far different from the basketball or horseback riding Kay used to do at home. In the third letter, Kay was
homesick. She missed her family and horses. She had promised
the minister at home that she would stay a month to give college
a fair try. The church members had taken up a special collection
to help pay her way, so she couldn't let them down, either.

Late one afternoon as we drove home from a dairy seminar
in Augusta, I said to Ron, "This is when I miss Kay the most.
Chores will be late tonight. It's four o'clock and we should have
been milking an hour ago."

As we came down the road toward the farm, I noticed the
lights were on in the barn. "Did you leave the lights on in the
barn this morning?" I asked.

"I don't think so," he replied. "Probably Darrell is graining
the cows."

We both saw her car at the same time.

"Kay's back!" I shouted. We hurried to the barn to see her.
There she was, dressed in jeans, sitting on the portable milking
stool, milking the cows.

Kay and Larry Seehafer back in Maine, 1988.

"Welcome home," I said as I grabbed Kay and hugged her. "Seems as though I've said that before."

"I hope you won't ever have to say it again," she said.

But then, a couple of years later, Kay gave her notice. She had become engaged to a man from New Hampshire and planned to move. She tried to talk him into moving to Maine, but he already had a good job in New Hampshire and wanted to stay. She told him she'd move only if she could take her horses with her. Soon after, Ron and I went to The County to visit my family for the weekend. When we returned home, Kyle announced that Kay had called off her wedding.

"She didn't ask, but I think she'd like to have her old job back," Kyle told us. "She said she'd be back in a few days."

"She can start tomorrow, as far as I'm concerned," Ron said. "We've got some second-crop hay to put in and we can use an extra pair of hands."

Several days later, Kay drove into the yard. "Welcome back!" I said as I grabbed Kay and hugged her. "Again!"

Kay settled down for several months but then grew restless yet again. Kay confided that she had a pen pal in Wisconsin named Larry Seehafer. She found him by reading an ad in *Hoard's Dairyman* that read, "Young Christian Farmer Wants to Meet Woman with Similar Interest. Willing to Travel to Meet Her." She had written to him and he had written back. She asked me not to tell anyone.

"I just mailed him a picture of myself and I'm waiting to get a picture of him," Kay said.

"Kay, he probably received letters from a hundred other girls," I said.

She smiled. "Larry sounds nice. He and his father have a herd of registered Holsteins and they classify, show and do embryo transfer work just like you do here."

"It's going to be hard to keep this a secret," I said.

A month later, Kay asked for the last two weeks of October off to visit Wisconsin and maybe look for a job.

This time when we hugged good-bye, I knew she wouldn't be back, at least not to work again. "I wish you the best of

The Seehafer family, 2001. Clockwise from the top is Larry, Kay, Troy, Tori, Carson, Sonya, and Eric. Tyler is in the middle.

everything, Kay," I said, trying to hold back the tears. "You deserve the best."

After a week, I looked for a letter every day. The days turned into weeks and still no letter. Finally, I couldn't stand the wait any longer and I called Kay's sister to get Kay's address. Dee told me that Kay had reached Wisconsin with twenty dollars in her pocket and took a job on a dairy farm in a town about twenty miles from Marathon. And she had met Larry.

"Why hasn't she written?" I asked.

"She hasn't written to anyone except my kids," Dee said. "My mother calls her once in a while to find out how she is."

Finally, a letter arrived after the holidays.

Kay was working with Larry on his farm and she liked his church. She said everything was going well. She and Larry were working hard. The herd had just been classified, and Larry had given her an embryo transfer calf that would be born in November. She wanted to come home in May for a visit, but probably couldn't afford it.

In March, Kay's mother called to tell us that Kay and Larry had eloped and would be home in the spring for a visit.

The next day Kyle received a birthday card. It was signed, Kay Seehafer.

The Cows are Out!

Twenty-One

A Bad Deal

We frequently attended cattle auctions and were always on the lookout for a cow with a good pedigree to improve herd genetics. We also sold cows at some auctions to raise money. One year we attended an auction at Little Willow Farm in Newcastle. Ron quickly showed me the cow he was interested in buying.

"How much do you think she'll sell for?" I asked, as we stood inspecting the huge, mostly black Holstein.

"She writes quite a pedigree and she'd make a good addition to our herd," Ron said. "I'm going to twenty-five hundred. With luck, she'll sell for less."

"If she sells for more, you're not going to bid, right?" I asked, demanding that his eyes meet mine. "You tend to get carried away at auctions."

As we walked behind a line of cows that had been washed and clipped for auction, I wondered how the owner felt about selling cows that he had bred and raised, cared for, and milked for thirty years. Even though we were buying, I hoped that the cows sold well.

As we studied pedigrees on other cows, Al Bates, who worked for the Holstein-Friesian Association of America, approached us. "Got your cow all picked out?" he asked.

"As a matter of fact, I do," Ron said. "She's number three, the big black one down the line."

"You and everyone else," Al replied. "I think she'll sell for big money. If you really want to buy one today, you'd better have a couple others in mind."

Al asked Ron if he wanted to go halves on number sixteen. We'd get her milk and then we'd split the income from her offspring. Ron liked that idea.

Other buyers from as many as one hundred farms across the Northeast studied their catalogs and milled around the old barn, stooping to study udders and stepping up beside cows to measure their heights.

A giant blue and yellow auction tent shaded the buyers from the July sun as they gathered and took seats, chatting about the cows and marking their catalogs.

"Let's get started," the auctioneer announced into his microphone from the platform at the front of the tent. "We've got some great cattle to sell here today and I know how anxious you are to start bidding. So, let's begin with this beautiful, big black cow from a family of high producers, high butterfat, longevity, and good udders. She can be yours today — so what do you say, let's start her out at two, yes, two and who'll give me three, who'll give me three?"

"Two hundred," I whispered in Ron's ear, "maybe we have a chance at her."

"Not two hundred," he said. "Two thousand."

"Two thousand! Are you sure?"

"Listen and find out."

Looking from the barn ell into the main barn at Craneland Farm. Every cow has a nametag over her with milk production and classification scores.

"I don't hear two," the auctioneer continued. "Well, then we'll start her off at fifteen, if that'll please you. How about fifteen? Do I hear fifteen? Yes! She's off and rolling, give me sixteen, yes, seventeen, now eighteen, now two. Yes! Do I hear twenty-two?"

"He's going up two hundred at a time now, are you going to bid?" I asked. Ron squirmed and cleared his throat. Beads of perspiration covered his brow.

"Okay, twenty-four, now twenty-six." The auctioneer's voice pitched higher with each increased bid. Ron didn't even have a chance to raise his hand before the bids went past the twenty-five hundred mark.

"Let's hear three," the auctioneer shouted, "now thirty-two, who'll give thirty-two?"

"Guess we won't buy her," Ron said, settling back into his chair.

"Thirty-five once, thirty-five twice. . . ." He banged his gavel on the podium. "Sold! Thirty-five hundred dollars!"

We looked around to see who had bought "our" cow. "Looks like the investment group from New York bought her," Ron said, as we watched a man in a three-piece suit sign the voucher slip.

"Do you want to try for number sixteen, the one Al said he'd go halves on with us?" I asked.

"I guess so," Ron replied. "Al said he'd put up a thousand for his half."

This time the bidding went our way. Soon, we had our new cow, and that afternoon we loaded Lotta onto the cattle truck.

"Eighteen hundred wasn't bad, was it?" I said. "We came prepared to spend twenty-five hundred and only used nine hundred."

"We'll see when we get her home," Ron replied. "She's dry right now, so she'll go out to pasture with the other dry cows until fall."

Lotta gave birth to a bull calf and entered the milking string.

"I hate this cow," Ron said as he milked Lotta for the third lactation. When he moved closer to her, she sidestepped away from him. As he placed his portable strap-on stool closer to her, Lotta stepped toward him, pushing him off balance.

"Looks as though the feeling is mutual," I said.

"I wish I'd never bought this bitch," he complained. Lotta had given birth to three bulls in a row, and during her last dry period, she came down with mastitis in one quarter, and as a result produced milk in only three quarters instead of four. Lotta turned and eyed Ron before lifting her tail and depositing runny manure that spattered Ron, the cow next to her, and the milking machine. Ron jumped up and reached for the hoe.

"She shits every time I come near her and she does it at least three or four times while I'm milking her."

"But she gives a lot of milk," I said, "as much as most cows give from four quarters."

Just as Ron started to scrape the manure from under Lotta, she kicked straight out, barely missing his arm.

"Look at that, she's half horse, too!" he yelled.

Lotta shivered as Ron bent over to remove the milking machine.

"If I didn't own her with Al Bates, I'd sell her in a minute. Better still, I'd beef her because I wouldn't wish her on anyone else. She's vicious, she's mean and she doesn't like people."

"We should keep her at least until she has a heifer calf," I said. "Otherwise, Al will never get his investment back."

Several months later we had to clip our cows' coats in preparation for an upcoming classification, an important rating of our cows that affected their value. The Holstein-Friesian Association of America sponsors an official classification program that farmers and owners of purebred Holstein cattle can participate in, if they pay a fee. Each cow is judged by an assigned classifier on body conformation and given a score (one hundred points for a "perfect" cow). The score is stamped on her registration paper. The higher the score, the more valuable and desirable both the cow and her offspring become, meaning they can potentially bring a higher sale price. The classification took place once a year.

"Does Lotta give you trouble when you milk her?" I asked Kay one afternoon.

"You mean 'Lotta shit'?" Kay asked.

I laughed. "I know about that, but does she kick or step on you?"

"She's nervous and I tiptoe around her so she doesn't get riled up. Why?"

"She has to be clipped for classification and I'm not sure I want to do it. Do you?"

"I'm not crazy about it, but I will if I have to."

"Look at her," I said. "We're three cows away from her and she's already treading."

When Ron entered the barn to check our progress, he said, "Don't clip Lotta. I'll clip her myself because I'm afraid she'll hurt someone."

Kay looked at me with raised eyebrows. Lotta watched Ron as he went to the other end of the barn to get a pair of clippers. She shifted back and forth in her stall as he oiled the clippers and plugged them into the extension cord. As he stepped into the stall beside her, she did what she was famous for — deposited manure. When Ron turned the clippers on, she swung her body away from him, slammed into the cow next to her, and violently lashed her tail.

"I'll show this cow who's boss," he said as he tied her tail to her front leg with a piece of baling twine. I got the hoe and scraped back the manure.

"Please try to stay calm," I said.

When he turned on the clippers a second time, Lotta threw her head away from him and swung her body in his direction, pinning him against the stanchion.

"You are a miserable old bag!" Ron shouted. "I'm going to clip you if it's the last thing I do." With all his might he shoved Lotta sideways. Lotta made another nervous deposit under her.

"Stay there," I said to Ron. "I'll scrape her back."

"No, I'll do it myself," he grumbled. "She may as well accept the fact that it's me and that I'm going to clip her."

For the third time Ron turned on the clippers and touched them to Lotta's side. She shivered, looked around at him with wild eyes, and struck at him with her foot.

"You want to kick me?" he said. "I'll fix you." Lotta watched every move as Ron went to the cabinet and took out the nose lead. She relaxed a little until she saw him approaching her head. She tried to dodge his efforts to get his arm around her neck, but he persisted until he finally inserted the nose lead into her nostrils. He pulled her head forward and tied the rope tightly to the scuttle ladder.

"Maybe that'll take your mind off kicking," he said.

He began with several short strokes on her side. Carefully, Ron was working his way down to her belly when Lotta exploded. She kicked the clippers from Ron's hand and sent them flying across the barn floor.

"That does it!" Ron raged. He stormed to the front of Lotta's stall and stood on the rope that held her nose. "How do you like that?" he asked, bouncing up and down on the rope. Then he leaned down and faced Lotta, nose to nose.

"What's he doing?" I asked as Kay and I walked up behind Lotta.

Ron marched back to where the clippers lay, picked them up, stepped up beside Lotta and began to clip. She continued to tread and kicked occasionally, but Ron kept on clipping nonstop.

"What did you do to her?" I asked.

"I bit her."

"You *what*?"

"I bit her, right on the nose. Look for yourself."

Kay and I went to the front of Lotta's stall and looked. There were his teeth imprints in Lotta's wet, shiny, nose. She licked the blood as it trickled over her nostrils.

"Why did you bite her?" I asked.

"Because if I hadn't bit her, I would have killed her!"

Three years later, we finally sold Lotta at auction. She fetched only seven hundred dollars. We sent half of it to Al Bates with our apologies for not making money for him on his investment.

TWENTY-TWO

A Show Cow

I named her Craneland Hetty Alyce Majesty. As a newborn, she was bigger than some two-month-old calves. And we were glad to get a heifer out of her aging dam, Alyce, because when a cow gets to be ten years old, one can't count on many more calves.

There is an official naming structure for registering Holsteins, which is why her name was so long. The Holstein-Friesian Association of America requires that names be no longer than thirty letters and spaces, and they must start with our registered prefix, Craneland, which no one except family members may use. Following the prefix is the calf's name, the dam's short name, and the sire's short name.

Besides her size and stature, Hetty was beautifully marked with nearly equal amounts of large patches of black and white. When I rubbed under her neck, she held her chin high. When I fed her milk, she leaned against me. She soon became my favorite.

Every Saturday morning, Ron let Hetty loose in the nursery while he shoveled out her pen and put fresh sawdust into it. Twice daily on other days of the week, we added fresh sawdust to the top layer. One day, I was feeding hay to the cows when I heard the crash and tinkle of glass. I ran to the nursery and found Ron leaning out the window.

"Hetty just did a long jump right out through the window," Ron said. "No horse could have done it better."

I thought she had probably broken her legs. It was a six-foot drop to the ground and there was an old bathtub lying upside down under the window. We ran out to see if she were injured and found her strolling in the belly-high grass in back of the barn.

"Not a scratch on her," Ron said. "Guess I'll tie her up next time."

"Did something scare her?" I asked.

"I don't think so," Ron replied. "I was shoveling sawdust into her pen when she tore by me as if she were running a steeplechase."

I knew Hetty would make a winning show calf, but we didn't have time to get her ready for the shows. Show season coincides with very busy seasons on the farm — summer and fall. We gave up showing unless it was a special occasion or cow. In general, it had become too stressful to take time away from essential chores to train a calf to lead, then practice leading her, wash, clip and transport her to a show, and then spend additional time away to show her.

But Hetty was special. Ron suggested that I enter her in the Futurity Show, a state show in which calves are entered at three months and then finally judged as milking two-year-olds. The entry fee was three dollars. If you thought the cow looked promising after six more months, you paid another fee of four dollars, or you could drop the entry. The last fee of ten dollars was due just before the show. The winners shared the pool money.

Photo by Mark Jenson

Craneland Hetty Alyce Majesty and me.

I decided to try it, hoping that we could manage one show a year, especially one in the fall after haying was done.

A short time later, our neighbor, Phil, and his daughter, Adrienne, called on us looking for a 4-H calf to lease for show season. County 4-H club members decide which events they will attend to show their cattle. They might attend as many as eight to ten shows, including state agricultural fairs and county shows during the summer and fall.

Because Hetty was sharp-looking and big for her age, Adrienne noticed her immediately. I took Hetty out of her pen so Adrienne could get a better look at her.

"Hi, Hetty," Adrienne cooed as Hetty immediately went to her and nuzzled her leg. "I think she likes me," Adrienne said.

She smiled and kneeled to put her arms around Hetty's neck. "Dad, this is the one."

Two weeks before the first show at the Bangor State Fair, Adrienne and her father came to pick up Hetty. Adrienne needed at least two weeks to train Hetty to lead with a halter, stop on command, hold her head and place her feet in a desirable position to be judged. She needed to wash her and clip her and become as friendly with her as possible.

I told Adrienne that some of our heifers had contracted ringworm. That day I had noticed a small spot on Hetty's neck. I advised Adrienne to watch Hetty carefully because she wouldn't be allowed in the show if she had ringworm.

The small spot on Hetty's neck was indeed ringworm and it spread to her face. Every day Adrienne scraped the spots with an iodine solution and applied antifungal cream to help dry up the fungus before show time. She also brushed the spots with vinegar and water to promote hair growth.

One winter our herd contracted ringworm. Every morning we put a halter on each cow and scraped the scaly sores until they bled and then applied iodine. Our vet warned us that ringworm was contagious and advised us to wash thoroughly after scraping the sores. Even though we followed his advice, Ron and I still contracted ringworm. Ron's started on his hands, which were difficult to treat because the salve wore off quickly. It crept into the cracks and calluses and spread under the outside layer of skin. Ron's hands, already thickly calloused with deep cracks around his nails from work were made even more sore. Eventually, he temporarily lost the skin on the palms of his hands.

After our annual physicals that year, Dr. Whitney and I returned to the waiting room, where Ron sat reading. "Trudy is in excellent health, except for one small thing," he reported.

"What's that?" Ron asked.

"She has a spot of ringworm on her buttock," he said with a smile. I blushed, trying to ignore the people who looked up from their magazines.

"She probably caught it from me," Ron said. "I just got over it."

"And where did you have it?" Dr. Whitney asked, still smiling.

They both chuckled. I turned to the receptionist and dug into my purse for a check.

"My hands," Ron replied, holding them up and smiling.

Hetty's ringworm healed past the contagious stage in time for Adrienne to take her to the Bangor State Fair.

Adrienne said Hetty was the easiest heifer she'd ever worked with. Hetty even followed Adrienne without a halter, which was fortunate in that Adrienne hadn't had much time to practice leading her.

As Adrienne led Hetty into the ring of junior calves, she looked around at the audience and smiled at her aunt and cousins. I tried to mentally guide her through the event. Come on, Adrienne, I thought, pay attention. Hold Hetty's head up. Adrienne continued around the ring nonchalantly, talking to Hetty and scratching her neck. Rattle the halter chain, Adrienne. Whistle at her, do something, I thought. It was difficult to tell who was leading whom, but Adrienne was pleased to place third in her class.

Girl and heifer became one that summer. They won enough shows to qualify for the Eastern States Exposition in Springfield, Massachusetts, that September. Hetty placed second in her class.

The next summer, the Waldo Holstein Breeders Club sponsored a cattle show at nearby Gold Top Farm. I thought we could make it a family affair. With the boys now in their late teens, I wondered if that was still possible.

Kyle didn't like the idea because he didn't think there was enough time to prepare, but Travis volunteered to lead Hetty in the show.

Hetty won the Junior Yearling Class and a trophy as Junior Champion at the Waldo County Show. This renewed Travis's enthusiasm for showing, so he took Hetty to the state show two weeks later, where she placed tenth. The judge said she had a thick neck and was a bit over-conditioned, but Hetty enjoyed every minute of Travis's clipping, washing, and primping. She strutted along in the ring as if she knew that she was special.

Hetty was bred to calve in July. Just before that, I led her in the Waldo County Show to practice for the Futurity Show in September. I had never shown before, and I was glad that Hetty was already trained. All I had to do was hold her head high and place her feet in the proper position when she stopped in the ring. Occasionally, she licked my arm or asked to be scratched under the chin. Two weeks later Hetty delivered a heifer calf that looked like her carbon copy. I named her Craneland Joan Hetty Valiant.

The day before the Futurity Show, I washed and clipped Hetty, leaving only the final touches until just before show time. Hetty and I rode to the Cumberland Fairgrounds with my neighbor, Margaret, who had entered three animals in the show.

"Bring warm clothes and a sleeping bag," Margaret said. "We'll be sleeping in the stalls with the cows."

Did she say sleep? I pondered that as I lay on the canvas cot that I thought would be more comfortable than hay. The cows had been milked, fed, watered, and bedded down for the night. I was warm, fed, and bedded down, but sleep did not come. The

Ferris wheel lights reigned over the midway and young voices and the smell of French fries filled the night air. The breathing, munching, and stirring of the cows were familiar and comforting, but the bleating of sheep and the squealing of pigs in the next shed were unfamiliar and annoying. Each time I dozed, the bleating and squealing woke me. I was awake when Margaret's alarm clock rang at three-thirty the next morning. The Ferris wheel was dark, and the young voices had ceased, but the smell of French fries lingered. The cows were standing and ready to be fed and milked. We moved about silently in the gray morning. Margaret gathered the portable milking equipment and I grained the cows and shoveled manure.

It *was* necessary to get up so early. The show wasn't until four o'clock that afternoon, but the cows needed to have at least twelve hours of milk in their udders to look their best. I had washed Hetty before leaving home, but decided that she could use another bath after the trip. Margaret agreed to help me clip Hetty, because I had never clipped for a show before.

After I washed and blanketed Hetty, I tied her in the end stall and tossed her a biscuit of second-crop alfalfa hay. She's beautiful, I thought, as I looked down the line of cattle. She's taller, her white is whiter, and her black shinier and her head prouder. When she was dry, I removed the blanket, brushed her and combed out her tail. People even began to gather around her, pointing and looking at the name tag posted above her.

Margaret and I took turns throughout the day feeding, watering, and shoveling so the cows stayed clean until show time. Hetty's udder filled with milk and she looked even better. Some of the same people who had admired her earlier came back to look at her again.

As show time neared, the show people, dressed in their white clothes and numbered hats, scurried to put the finishing touches on their cows. They snipped stray hairs from the backs, wiped baby oil over the shoulders for extra shine, brushed the hooves, and teased the tails.

When the announcer called for the Junior Two-Year-Old Class, I removed Hetty's rope halter and put the black leather show halter on her. As I turned to lead her out of the stall, Hetty bolted and mounted the cow beside her.

"Get down!" I screamed. The cow being ridden stepped aside and Hetty slid off the cow's rump, landing on my right foot. I grimaced with pain and leaned my head against Hetty's side.

"I think Hetty's in heat," Margaret said. "Are you okay?"

"I'm so tired and numb by now, I don't know," I answered.

"You had better hang back and enter the ring last or you may have trouble holding her," Margaret advised. "Keep a fair distance or she will try to mount the cow in front of you."

I limped as I led Hetty out into the path en route to the ring. She stretched her neck and sniffed the passing cows and reared up several times. Just what I need the first time out, I thought. Hetty, usually so easy to lead, strained at the halter and tested every muscle in my arms.

As I neared the ring, Ron and Kyle arrived. "How are you doing?" Ron asked.

"Terrible," I said. "Would you like to lead Hetty? She's in heat and acting awful."

"At least she'll be alert," Ron laughed. "You're going to be fine. Just keep your distance from the cow in front of you."

The judge observed each cow as it was led into the ring. I entered last. The judge asked questions, felt the cows' hides, and bent to look closely at the udders.

"When did she calve?" the judge asked as he studied Hetty.
"July," I said nervously.
"Quite alert today, isn't she?" he commented.
"She's in heat," I said.
He smiled as he waved me by.

I had circled only once when the judge motioned me to the center of the ring. I knew that the one called first into the center of the ring takes first place. The judge may rearrange the other placings, but he seldom changes first place. At that moment, Hetty tossed and threw her head down, jerking my arms toward the ground. I snapped the chain under her chin and yanked her head up. "Be good, Hetty," I said to her. "Can't you see he likes us?"

The judge was busy placing the rest of the entries as I led Hetty to the middle of the ring and tried to place her feet in the proper show position. She shook her head and sidestepped, bumping the second-place cow that the judge had motioned in beside her. "Sorry," I said, "my cow is in heat." I tightened the chain on the halter and pulled Hetty's head around. We jockeyed back and forth until she quieted. Her feet weren't in perfect position, but I decided to leave well enough alone.

After seeing the animals posed side by side, the judge changed his mind about several of his placings and rearranged them, glancing back at Hetty occasionally. "We've got it made now," I whispered to her, scratching her neck. Right then and there I forgot about my sleepless night and forgave Hetty for stepping on my foot — we had won the blue ribbon.

I finally relaxed enough to look down the line of other winners — the premier breeders in the state. Hetty was the best and most beautiful cow in the ring.

I looked at Ron and Kyle, who grinned from ear to ear and gave me the thumbs-up sign.

"We did it, Hetty, we won!" I said to her as I led her out of the ring. Ron was there to take the halter and I lowered my arms in relief. "Am I glad that's over," I said. "She was almost too much for me to handle."

But it wasn't over. Ron informed me that after the Senior Two-Year-Old Class is judged, the top five in each class return to the ring for the final placings. I had to do it all over again, knowing that juniors don't usually place first overall because they are younger.

Hetty placed fourth in the final judging. After she was covered with a show blanket, I looked up at the three top placings — all seniors — and then down the line at the six below us.

"Today, Hetty," I whispered in her ear, "you are the fourth-best cow in the entire state of Maine."

TWENTY-THREE

Launching a Holiday Tradition

It was my idea to put a lighted tree on top of our seventy-foot Harvestore silo. I thought something so out of the ordinary would surely liven up the holiday season, and it was an inexpensive way to cheer people. My family was not so thrilled with the idea.

The little girl in me still found magic in holiday lights. I loved getting the tree into the house early so I could enjoy it for several weeks before Christmas. I'd lie on the couch and dream back to when I knew for certain there would be a new doll under the tree — every single Christmas until I was fifteen. For me, the tree lost its magic as soon as the gifts were opened, although I kept it in the house well into January. And now, the idea of a lighted tree on top of the silo — awesome!

After suggesting several more times that we put a tree on the silo, Ron and the boys finally agreed to do it if I would help.

"I'll buy the lights and help pick out a tree," I said enthusiastically.

"That's not the sort of help we had in mind," Ron replied. "We want you to actually help put the tree up there."

"You mean climb up the silo?" I asked. They nodded in unison.

They knew I was afraid of heights. They'd been trying for years to get me up on that silo but I had no desire to do so. In the fall, after the silo was full, someone had to climb to the top and sweep off the haylage that accumulated as it was blown into the top pipe (this was basically for esthetics — there was no actual need to do this). I couldn't even watch as Ron, Kyle or Travis, tied with a rope from his waist to the rail around the catwalk, walked out onto the slanted silo top and swept it clean, let alone do it myself.

"Mom, you would be so glad if you did it," Kyle coaxed. "The view is great. You can see all around, for miles. Come on, won't you?"

"No, I won't," I replied, "and I'll take your word about the view. Besides, I think it's mean of you to try to bribe me just because you know how much I want a tree up there."

"Think of it as a challenge," Ron said.

I thought about the tree for several days. Then I purchased the lights — four strings of twenty-five each. At supper I announced that I had bought the lights and that I would help put up the tree. They seemed surprised and I'm not certain they believed me. Secretly I thought that surely if they took time to cut a tree and I helped with the preparations, they wouldn't back out at the last minute if I refused to climb the silo. Would they?

When my parents arrived for Thanksgiving, I told them about our plan.

"Quite an ambitious project, isn't it?" my father asked. I knew by his voice that the idea intrigued him.

After Thanksgiving dinner, we went to the pasture and chose a large tree. Then, with my father directing from below,

The lights from our outside Christmas tree high atop one of the farm's silos could be seen for miles.

Kyle and Travis tied a pulley to the top of the silo and looped a rope through it. At the bottom, Ron tied the tree to one end of the rope and the other end to the bucket of the tractor. As I backed the tractor slowly away from the silo, the tree rose to the top. That was the easy part. I was relieved that the tree was

159

finally up there and I had not been asked to climb. Using the rope and pulley, we sent up a bucket filled with four strings of lights. Then Ron climbed the sixty-five-foot ladder on the side of the silo. He and the boys attached the lights and wired the tree upright to the rails of the catwalk. It was not yet dark when Dad and I connected several extension cords and plugged them into a barn outlet to check for broken or burned-out bulbs.

"Mom," Kyle shouted down, "where are the spare bulbs?"

"In my pocket. Do you need some?"

"Yes," he answered. "Bring them up."

"Who, *me?*"

"Yes, Mom. Come on."

He's got me now, I thought. I should have gone back to the house after the tree was up. I drew a deep breath, reached for the ladder and slowly placed my foot on the bottom rung. I stopped and looked up, even though there was a cage all around me, my heart was pounding.

"Don't look up, Mom," Travis advised. "Just look at each step as you go. You can do it."

I took several more steps up and looked down. "Don't look down, either," Kyle said.

"What if I fall?" I asked.

"You can't fall," Kyle said. "We need the bulbs if you want this tree to look pretty."

I kept climbing, but to this day, I don't know how I did it. When I reached the top, I peeked up over the edge of the silo. I clung, white-knuckled, with one hand on the top rung. With the other hand, I reached into my pocket for the spare bulbs. Without looking up, I held them up over the edge. "This is the top, up here where we are," Kyle insisted.

"If I go up over the edge, I'll never be able to back off onto the ladder again," I said. "If you want these bulbs, you'll have to come here and get them because I'm not going one more inch."

Without looking sideways, I started my slow descent, exhausted when my feet finally touched the ground again.

"I did it," I said to my father. "My first and last trip up the silo."

After dark we all piled into my father's car. First we drove to the top of The Ridge, and then we went in four different directions to admire the lighted Christmas tree from every possible vantage point. We received so many favorable comments, including those in letters from people we didn't even know, that when the holidays rolled around again, we put up another tree. Ron and Kyle did the job with my mother fretting, unable to watch, and my mother-in-law peering out the window every few minutes, predicting that someone would fall.

The third year, fall work ran into winter and there didn't seem to be time to put up the tree. After Christmas, Ron remarked, "You wouldn't believe how many people have asked why we didn't put a Christmas tree on the silo this year. Guess we'll have to make it a priority for next year."

The fourth year Kyle and a college fraternity brother launched the tree.

Several days after the lighting, we received a letter from a neighbor, eight-year-old Lynn Keller. She thanked us for putting the tree up again and said how she had missed it the year before.

"How can we not keep on doing it?" Ron asked after reading her letter. "Looks as though it has become a Christmas tradition."

The fifth year wasn't as easy. Kyle had lost his enthusiasm. Ron reminded him that we had started a tradition, so with persuasion and the luck of an unseasonably warm day the first week of December, Kyle gave in. Berna, our second Saint Bernard, watched curiously while we "dressed" the tree on the ground and snugged the branches together with rope. Before launching the tree, we plugged in the lights to test for burned-out bulbs. Berna barked her approval.

When the tree was in place on top of the silo and the lights turned on, I remarked to Kyle how beautiful it looked. "I probably wouldn't have agreed to it," he said, "except Dad says it makes you happy."

It did make me happy, and a lot of other people, too. Maine winters are long, and the tree was a cheerful sight when I headed out to the barn in the early morning darkness of December.

TWENTY-FOUR

The First Taste of Spring

I had my own fiddlehead patch, making me one of the luckiest people in the state of Maine. My favorite food since early childhood has been steamed fiddleheads with butter and salt. Growing up in Aroostook County, I considered eating fiddleheads, usually picked by my grandfather, part of an annual spring ritual. I just took them for granted. Of course today, fiddleheads are considered a delicacy in many fine restaurants.

As an adult, I always shared my harvest of fiddleheads with friends and relatives, but I have shared my fiddlehead patch with only four other people — besides my husband — whom I trusted to keep the secret. Never ask anyone to reveal the location of her fiddlehead patch.

My neighbor actually gets the credit for discovering it. He noticed the ferns in the woods on Beaver Hill when he was installing drainage tile in fields that we were preparing to seed down by plowing, harrowing, and picking rocks. Although it was too late to harvest the fiddleheads that spring, I was forever beholden to him for his discovery.

One May, according to my calendar, fiddlehead season had arrived. It was my morning off from barn chores but I still awoke at 5:00 A.M., so I decided to go fiddleheading. I should have known by the absence of blackflies that the fiddleheads weren't quite ready. I went anyway because I didn't want one sprout of the succulent wild vegetable to get ahead of me. My suspicions were right — not one fiddlehead had yet poked through the brown root mounds.

After two warm, rainy days, the blackflies were out. I visited my patch again. Eureka! The fiddleheads were up — meaning mossy-green, quarter-sized coils stood ready on three-inch stems. I came home with a small mess of Mother Nature's first taste of spring.

On my third trip to the patch, the fresh air felt cool against my face. Along the dirt road to the alfalfa field, the hazy sunshine filtered long early morning shadows through the baby green leaves. The first dandelion blossoms — whose greens are the first taste of spring for some people — fringed the rock wall that I stepped across. New alfalfa had started to grow, but last year's dry stubble crunched under my boots as I hiked toward the woods with my plastic shopping bags and a bottle of fly repellent, just in case. No blackflies in sight. I was up before them.

I stepped into the woods and saw that some ferns had unfurled their heads. In just a few days, those exposed to sunshine had grown knee high and were too tall to pick. But there in the shade beside the spring brook grew the perfect green clumps. I began grabbing handfuls, seven or eight stalks at a time.

Why was I hurrying? I had no deadlines this morning and there were enough fiddleheads to fill two shopping bags. Still, I continued to pick full tilt, wanting to harvest the stalks before they could grow any bigger. All the while I took care not to step

Photo by Stephen Leighton

Fiddleheads ready for spring harvest!

on some jack-in-the-pulpits that thrived in the same damp environment as fiddleheads. I didn't even stop to wipe the drip on the end of my nose. Leaving the taller stems to become ferns, I invaded the middle section of shorter plants, plucking out the tenderest and tastiest morsels that had barely popped through their brown skins.

Two hours and two bags full of fiddleheads later, I realized that I had not yet spoken to anyone this morning, and no one had spoken to me except Old Sam Peabody whose song I returned by whistling. With regret that a few fiddleheads had outgrown my picking and a promise to those not yet through their brown skins that I would return, I left my favorite spot to go cook breakfast for my family.

As I walked from the woods, the first morning blackflies buzzed my head and a crow squawked from his perch. On the way home I left my friend Mattie enough fiddleheads for dinner and later dropped some off for my sister-in-law.

The rest I would put in the freezer for special occasions such as Thanksgiving, Christmas, Easter or when we had guests. If they had never tasted Maine's delicacy, I made certain that our guests were in another room when I drained the brown water from the cooking pot. If they were hesitant about tasting the curious coiled young fronds, the brown water might increase their hesitancy.

For several days after the picking, my green-stained fingers and nails would remind me of the bountiful excursion and the solitude of my fiddlehead patch — no telephone, no calves blatting for morning milk, no manure to shovel. My back complained, but my soul had been revitalized for at least another week.

TWENTY-FIVE

Getting Up with the Cows

I wasn't always a morning person. And only former night people can understand how difficult it is to change. Although, if anything can change a night person into a morning person, it's dairy farming.

Ideally, cows should be milked every twelve hours. When we bought our farm, Ron continued the existing routine — milking at four in the morning and three in the afternoon. (Ron's timing varied only slightly depending on the season.) This schedule allowed time for daily work, such as gardening, haying, spreading manure and repairing equipment. It also left time for supper and evening activities. Other farmers have their own schedules. We knew one old-timer who milked his cows at noon and midnight. He was a night person for sure.

I was born into a night family. We stayed up late — reading, studying, watching TV, knitting, sewing or playing cards. Ron was always a morning person and doesn't understand night people, so we had to make many adjustments over the years. In winter, when he arose at three o'clock (as opposed to three-thirty during the summer) to milk the cows, he was happy and often hummed, anticipating the day's activities. Right from the start, I discouraged the humming, as well as turning on the light at that hour. I considered three o'clock the middle of the night, not morning. At 5:00 A.M., I arose grudgingly to feed calves, sweep cribs and wash milking equipment. I didn't speak to anyone for at least an hour, and that was a good thing.

When I agreed to become a farmer, no one mentioned feeding calves at that hour of the morning. I wondered why calves must be fed exactly at five-thirty. It soon became obvious: completing the morning barn chores as soon as possible left more time during the day for additional work.

Physically, it didn't take many weeks of this routine to change me into a morning person. I simply had to go to bed early.

I also discovered that starting the day early had its advantages. Soon, I felt cheated if I didn't see the sunrise. It's the most peaceful time of day. The phone has yet to ring, traffic is at a minimum, and the air is usually fresh, cool, and clear. I actually started to converse with the other workers. Rising early kept my bodily functions in sync, toned my muscles and enhanced my appetite. By the time I had worked three or four hours in the barn, I looked forward to breakfast. When I was a night person, I never had an appetite in the morning.

I napped every chance I got, even if it was for only fifteen minutes. I used to think that any nap of less than two hours wasn't worth it. Forget that. Ron survived dairy farming because of his catnaps. I was concerned one day when he was mowing hay and didn't return for lunch, so I went to find him. As I drove into the field, I noticed that the tractor was stopped. When I got closer, I saw Ron lying underneath it. Fearing he had had an accident, I jumped out of the pickup truck and

Taking care of afternoon chores inside the barn, 1988.

shouted his name as I ran toward the tractor. My voice startled him from a sound sleep and he rose up suddenly and bumped his head on the underside of the tractor.

On an occasional morning off, Ron still awoke at three o'clock, but he rolled over and went right back to sleep. On my mornings off, I still awoke at 5:00 A.M. but seldom went back to sleep. During the twelve years I had my horse, Jud, I took advantage of the early daylight hours of spring to go for a ride. During the winter, I was able to catch up on household chores.

After finally becoming accustomed to my morning routines, I went to visit my mother in The County. She still sat up late and I tried to stay up with her and talk. The first evening, my eyelids got heavy about nine o'clock. The second night, I was able to stay up a bit later. Then by the fourth night, I joined my mother in watching the late news and sleeping in until nine or ten the next morning. It only took four days to become my old night self again. It was then I gave up any hope of ever becoming a true morning person.

Twenty-Six

A Pig Deal

I never believed in packing things away that are used at least once during the year. It always seems that as soon as you wash and put away the winter caps and coats, it comes off cold and you have to dig them out again. In the back hallway, I hung an all-season variety of outerwear. I also left hanging there painting pants used once each summer by Russ, a former college room-mate of Ron's.

"Price, when are you going to paint the barn trim?" Russ asked one early spring when he and Jan came for a visit.

"Oh, it's on my list," Ron assured him.

"How about I do it for you and you raise me a pig? I've been wanting to have my own pork for the freezer."

"Okay by me," Ron said, "but that's really my wife's department. She raises the pigs."

Ron and Russ always had a deal going. I married into those deals, so Russ and I always had a deal going, too.

Russ taught high school math in Massachusetts and did odd jobs during summer vacations. A trip to Maine served four-fold. He visited his parents and grandparents on Muscongus Bay, took wool from his sheep to Harmony Mills and exchanged it for yarn for Jan, enjoyed the farm and countryside, and visited us.

We all enjoyed those visits, talking over old college days and catching up on family happenings. Sometimes, Russ brought his sons, Lee and Clay, to stay the week on the farm. Then our boys returned with them to Massachusetts. Russ took them to Red Sox games at Fenway Park and made trips to the Museum of Science and the New England Aquarium. I doubt that Kyle and Travis would ever have seen a Red Sox game if it hadn't been for Russ.

A bit of a frustrated farmer, Russ dabbled in animal husbandry. Homing pigeons had been a hobby and source of income since he was a young boy. He earned his way through college by selling breeding stock and winning pigeon races. Besides the coop that his prized flock occupied behind his house, he used a barn and pasture across the road where he housed several sheep, a dozen hens, a Jersey cow, Satin, and her calf.

The deal I had with Russ this particular time was that in exchange for painting the barn trim, I agreed to raise him a pig up to one hundred pounds. I would get the pig in spring. Russ would come up as usual during the summer, this time to paint, and then he would take the pig back to Massachusetts. I justified the deal in my mind. I already had a pig and two pigs were as easy to raise as one. More fun, too. Painting around the farm was not so much fun, so the job was always placed at the end of a never-completed, overwhelmingly long list which Ron kept in several little notebooks all over the place.

This particular summer, Russ came to paint — not just visit. Before the actual painting began, we went out to the old chicken house where the two pigs had lived since May. Russ would be pleased with his pig, I thought. She was looking good — long, lean, pink, and clean. He trusted me to choose her from a litter owned by our veterinarian, George.

The pigs were lively, but tame. When Travis was a young boy, he had made pets of all the pigs we raised. He played peek-a-boo through the windows covered with chicken wire. During other games, he was careful to face their heads to avoid any playful bites. The most fun he had with the pigs was riding on their backs, trying to stay on as they weaved and twisted to dump him off — and not always on the clean side of the pen. Given ample room and bedding, pigs will use one side of a pen for a toilet and keep the other side clean for rest and sleep. Travis also noticed that pigs smile at other times besides when they sleep. They grinned from inside the windows when they saw him coming to play a game.

"You've done a great job," Russ praised me. "What's her name?"

"Oh, we never do that," I told him. "Pigs with names are harder to eat."

"I'd like to raise some piglets myself, but there's not a boar good enough for her down home."

Through George's hired worker, Tommy, Russ found a young boar that he thought would work well on his young sow. When Russ left a week later, he had Tommy's boar and his own sow loaded in the back of his pickup truck, which was fitted with six-foot-long side-boards all the way around.

It was sprinkling rain as we hugged and expressed wishes for a safe trip back. The pigs squeaked, snorted, and stamped in the back of the truck. Russ didn't plan to stop on his way back to Massachusetts, wanting to get his cargo to their new home as soon as possible.

As Russ hummed along the highway, the rain became heavier. It's a warm rain, he thought, the pigs shouldn't mind. He glanced occasionally at his sideview mirror and thought he saw a flash of something on the top of the side-boards. A nose? Couldn't be. Pigs can't jump that high. I probably imagined the nose, he thought. *Thunk!* Russ looked in the rearview mirror. A nose and a foot. That crazy pig! He slowed down. *Thunk! Crash!* A nose, two feet, and a head. Better pull over and see what's ailing those foolish pigs, Russ decided.

But before he could stop the truck, he saw the sow scrambling to her feet alongside the grassy embankment of the highway. The boar clunked against the cab of the truck as Russ came to a stop.

Believe it now, he said to himself. Pigs *can* jump six-foot side-boards. The cars whizzed by and Russ feared the sow would get run over. He sloshed along the roadside in pursuit of his pig. She seemed a bit stunned and staggered slightly from her fall, but she soon gathered herself and gained momentum.

While thoughts of a greased pig contest went through Russ's head, another pickup truck slowed and stopped. Out jumped a fellow who went right about chasing the pig without uttering a word. Pretty nice of him to help me catch my pig, Russ thought. He was immediately beholden to the helper as they weaved to and fro, slipping and sliding on the grass and rocks, while the runaway sow deftly dug in her hooves and dodged their attempts to capture her.

By now, the rain drizzled from Russ's beard and dripped from the helper's nose. Breathless, all three slowed and planned their next moves. Russ stalked the pig from the rear while the Good Samaritan approached her head slowly, stooping with his arms spread wide. The pig's final attempt at freedom failed as

Russ muckled onto her rear legs while the helper grabbed her front legs. All three sprawled to the ground, deafened by the pig's squeals.

"Sure was good of you to help me catch my pig," Russ panted.

"*Your* pig?" croaked the helper. "She's my pig. I was going to thank you."

"But she just jumped out of my truck back there," Russ said, nodding in the direction of his parked vehicle. "I have another one in there, look for yourself."

The young sow continued to struggle, her feet slipping and grating on the four hands that still held fast. Each man tugged firmly in his direction.

"Sure," the helper said sarcastically, "sure, she's your pig; sure, she jumped over six-foot side-boards. She's *my* pig, I tell you. Look over there."

He rolled over on his side and nodded. "See that place with the fenced-in yard? I have twenty-two pigs in there. If you don't believe me, let's go over there and count them."

"If you'll help me put this pig into the back of my truck, I'll be glad to follow you over to your place and count your pigs," Russ said.

They put the pig in the truck and Russ followed the helper across the road to his place. They counted twenty-two pigs, not once, but twice. The helper allowed that the high jumper must belong to Russ, since his own seemed to be accounted for.

"You'd have thought he'd have known right away that she wasn't his pig," Russ said when he related the tale to Ron over the phone that night. "His pigs were all different colors — spotted, black, brown and white — not near as pretty and pink and clean as mine."

"See you at the end of August," Ron ended the conversation.

"Why the end of August?" I asked, after Ron hung up.

"Russ is coming back to stain the new shingles on the barn ell. He thought it should be done this year."

"But we can't pay him," I objected.

Ron hesitated, then smiled. "Russ said to tell you that he thought you and he could work out a deal."

TWENTY-SEVEN

Eating Well

One benefit of dairy farming is the ability to raise some sort of critter for the freezer in the fall. Some were more desirable than others. Esther, an older cow, was the first. She had not conceived after repeated breeding and was going dry. Since she would never again be a productive dairy animal, we decided to have her slaughtered for meat and put into the freezer. At the time, our sons, Travis and Kyle, were two and four years old. They accepted the plan after some explanation and even ate the meat enthusiastically. I'm not sure how much they really understood. They saw Esther leave on the cattle truck and return in small, frozen, white-paper packages. Fortunately, they missed the in-between process.

Unlike many children, farm children learn at an early age the true origins of food, and it simply becomes part of life. Still, we did occasionally take steps to make it a little easier when an animal we raised was slaughtered. While cows require names to become registered with the Holstein-Friesian Association of America, we avoided naming our pigs other than "Pig" or "Pork." When the meat was finally in the freezer and the pork chops were served, it

Travis takes a joy ride.

was better if we weren't reminded that it was Petunia or Rosie that we were eating.

We also learned to avoid using certain animals for beef, such as older cows like Esther, and animals that had been stressed. After one heifer, named Trudy, had a difficult first delivery with a large bull calf, she ended up paralyzed in one leg and couldn't get up. When she didn't improve after several days, we decided to have her slaughtered for meat. But we couldn't eat the meat because it was tough and had an odd flavor. I learned two lessons: try to avoid eating meat from a stressed animal, and never name a heifer after myself.

We continued to learn from our trials and errors. We started to plan ahead — choosing a specific animal for a beef critter. One fall we went to the pasture to catch a steer that we had raised for beef. He was unfriendly and avoided our attempts to lure him with a bucket of grain into the trailer. After several hours of chasing him around the pasture, we finally succeeded in getting a halter on him and dragged him, inch by inch, into the trailer. Everyone, including the steer, was stressed and, true to form, it was the toughest meat we ever ate.

Once we raised a steer named Fred. Travis claimed Fred from the beginning, and they were special friends for two years. Fred lived a stress-free life. When Travis went to the pasture and called out, Fred ran over to the fence. Travis climbed onto Fred's back and off they trotted for a few turns around the pasture, like a horse and his favorite rider. When it was time for Fred to go for slaughter, we backed the trailer into the pasture and opened the tailgate. Reluctantly, Travis called and Fred trotted over and followed him into the trailer. It was a sad day. But Fred's easy life did lead to one great benefit at the supper table that told the full story: It was the most tender meat we ever ate.

THE COWS ARE OUT!

Twenty-Eight

A Record Day

The farm was a hazy blur as I looked back from the tractor seat. The hundred-foot barn and seventy-foot silo looked small. At 6:00 A.M. I felt as if I had never slept or left the tractor seat. When darkness overtook me the night before, the tractor lights were too dim and had cast shadows over the rows of mowed hay, forcing me to quit for the night.

"What am I doing here on this tractor?" I asked myself.

As a partner and co-worker on the farm, I had had my doubts about buying this huge, $10,000, secondhand, 105-horsepower Massey-Ferguson tractor. Concerned about how we would pay for it, I learned to drive it myself instead of hiring someone else. Driving your own tractor is best, anyway. An owner-driver tends to drive the tractor with more respect and attention to maintenance. Tractors are one of the few farm purchases that don't depreciate. Built to last, they may even increase in value, especially if well cared for.

Still, I doubted my ability to drive such an enormous piece of machinery. Our previous tractor was just 55-horsepower. Ron assured me I could drive it. He pointed out that the big tractor was safer because there was less chance of rolling over. And, I had a nice cab to protect me from the sun, wind and dust. It even had fans to keep me cool.

And drive it, I did. First, because of Ron's confidence in me, and second, because of self-confidence I had acquired after years of experience.

I looked around at our forty-acre field, the largest on the home place, and prepared to chop the mowed hay into haylage. The view of field, woods, and western mountains from Knox Ridge was breathtaking. What better place to spend the day in fresh air and sunshine? Ideally, haylage should be about 50 percent moisture for chopping and then blowing up the long pipe into the top of our Harvestore silo, a blue, seventy-foot tall, vacuum-sealed structure. The silo could hold seven hundred tons of haylage and we had purchased this "blue angel" secondhand for about $30,000 (requiring another FHA loan). Kyle and Travis thought it was wonderful that we got a "free" set of Harvestore salt and pepper shakers in the deal. I would only put one on the table for fear that putting them both out might mean getting a second silo.

This hay was damp and heavy to start, but as the day got hotter, it could become too dry for haylage. The previous day I had chopped twenty-five loads. There must be fifty loads in this field, I thought.

One of the trucks arrived to pick up a load. The two trucks looked identical but drove very differently, each requiring a special method of shifting gears and each with mechanical quirks to which my sons had become accustomed. Kyle drove "his" truck and Travis drove "his" truck; each performed his own maintenance, and they never swapped trucks.

Travis, especially, was very possessive of certain things, such as his truck and his chair at the table. Once, as a six-year-old, he

A spring view of Knox Ridge, 1990. Craneland Farm is in the center with Route 220 running past our front driveway. Our pasture is to the right and top of the farm, while our forty-acre hay field is to the left.

embarrassed our family as guests sat down to supper. One guest inadvertently chose Travis's place. Everyone sat down except Travis, who remained standing. He glared in the direction of "his" chair. "Come sit by me," I suggested. "That's my chair," he blurted to the innocent interloper who occupied his usual place. There was a shuffling of chairs while we rearranged the seating to accommodate Travis.

From the tractor seat I controlled the hydraulic dump wagon with levers that lifted it high into the air so five tons of beautiful green haylage fell into the truck. With all going smoothly and both boys hauling, I chopped a load every fifteen minutes.

When Kyle arrived, I told him that the reverse feed-roll on the chopper wasn't working. When working properly, it allows the operator to release wads of grass that sometimes wind

183

Night Work. Here I am dumping another load of haylage, 1986.

around the intake feed-roll instead of passing, as it should, into the blower of the chopper. Kyle had a serious expression on his face and his immediate attack on the breakdown was typical. Sometimes we hesitated to tell him about small problems because his conscientiousness could drive him to turn a minor adjustment into a time-consuming major overhaul. Travis nicknamed his brother "Major." Previously, he had been "Captain Kyle" because he excelled at bossing and overseeing his younger brother's activities. But Travis promoted Kyle from Captain to Major when Kyle became old enough to perform major repairs and maintenance on farm equipment.

At age three, Kyle already knew he wanted to be a dairy farmer like his dad. After high school, he wanted to stay at home and farm, but because he had always been an honor student, we encouraged him to continue his education. He enjoyed so many other interests that I thought he might lose his enthusiasm for farming at college; instead, his determination only grew stronger. He graduated from the University of Maine in 1985 with degrees in animal science and agricultural mechanization, and he came home to farm.

He checked out the machine and I was relieved that a simple clutch adjustment on the chopper solved the problem.

Getting our hay in wasn't always this easy. When we baled our hay, rather than chopped it for haylage, it took more time and effort. In ideal weather, preparing hay to be baled took at least two or three days to dry to 25 percent or less moisture. It required mowing, tedding (spreading it out), raking, and baling — four trips over the field with a tractor, mower, tedder and rake, besides hauling it on trailers to the farm, unloading it, and stacking it in the barn.

In comparison, haylage could be mowed, chopped, and blown into the silo, sometimes the same day (although it was usually the next day), even in cloudy weather. It required only two trips over the field with a tractor, thereby saving half the fuel, and half as many people could do the job. The trend toward wetter Junes and the ease of handling haylage were the reasons we changed our first crop from baled hay to haylage.

When we started farming in 1966, baled hay, along with commercially mixed grain, was the only forage fed to the cows. Because our farm lacked haying equipment, we hired Ron's cousin, Dick, to custom-harvest the hay, and Ron worked for him. It seemed as though we baled hay all summer. By the time we finished the last field of first crop, the first field was ready to be cut again for second crop. But with haylage and a silo, four people could work the entire operation: Ron mowed, I chopped, and the boys hauled and blew it into the silo. Haylage cut in early June contains up to 19 percent protein and is extremely palatable to cows. Half of a percent of protein is lost every day the haylage is not harvested after June 15. Since baled hay can rarely be harvested before then, early-cut haylage gives the farmer higher-quality forage.

Kyle's girlfriend and future wife, Karen, was living with us that summer. Karen, a senior at the University of Maine majoring in general agriculture, would bring lunch to the field and have supper ready when we finished. I truly enjoyed field work when I didn't have to return to housework and preparing meals afterward. I ate a donut and drank iced tea between loads.

The herring gulls made shadows on the ground ahead of me like airplanes flying too low. A gray dust followed the tractor as Ron mowed the rest of the long field below the rock wall. Twenty-two loads so far this day. The record for a twenty-four-hour period was thirty-three loads.

Travis returned and positioned his truck parallel and within a few inches of the dump wagon. He grinned at me. He was shirtless and his rugged shoulders were tanned. He held up the new issue of *Hot Rod* magazine that came in the noon mail. As I dumped the load of haylage into his truck, he scanned the pages and held up a full-page picture of a motorcycle. I hoped that he was teasing when he pointed to it and then to himself. He had already used up eight of his nine lives, two of them on motorcycles.

What a wonderful field this was to work — big, open, and near the farm in case of breakdowns. With few problem spots in the field, I had time to look around as I chopped. I noticed the rocks piled along the rock walls, some as small as eggs, hand-picked from the fields by the Vose family who had first worked this land. A rock wall can serve as a storage place for a multitude of items saved for future use. Old gutter cleaner chains, silo hoops, and old cedar fence rails and fence posts decorated our rock walls that were fringed with buttercups, daisies, and wild purple asters. One rock wall behind our barn had served several generations as a junkyard for discarded items that nowadays we would recycle or haul to the dump — bottles, cans, kettles, pieces and parts of mechanical devices. We leveled that wall with a bulldozer and covered it with gravel to use as a driveway and lane for the cows to go to the back pasture.

Unfortunately, our machines do upset Mother Nature. A mother wren was angry with me. She perched on the next unchopped row each time I eliminated one. She flitted, then stopped to search for her nest, lecturing me the whole time. "I'm sorry I've destroyed your nest," I said aloud. "Build it in a safer place next time."

Most animals were frightened away by the noise of the machinery. Snakes slithered toward the rock wall, woodchucks hid in their underground homes, rabbits sprung to the woods, mice leapt like kangaroos to any place at all. A toad moved slowly to the unchopped row each time I came around, each time endangering her life. Finally, I could ignore her no longer. I stopped the tractor, dismounted and, with my foot, urged her hop by hop to the rock wall on the edge of the field where she would be safe. With a clear conscience I continued my work. Many slaughters went unnoticed until the crows, gulls, and hawks swooped down to carry off their free meals. I tried not to feel guilty.

I turned my rig in the opposite direction to chop the outside windrow before it got too dry. As I turned the corner, I adjusted the spout on the chopper with the electric controls so that the stream of haylage entered the wagon; otherwise, it shot up into the air, fell onto the ground, and was wasted. As I straightened the rig and pulled the lever to center the spout, it remained pointed to the side.

After a quick survey, I realized it needed repair, so I stopped the tractor, trotted across the field, ducked under the electric fence, and went across the pasture to the farm shop. There, Ron was in the midst of a salesman's demonstration of an engine crane. Irritated that a salesman could be so inconsiderate as to interrupt a farmer's work on the best day of the summer, I was a bit short. "I'm broken down and need your help," I announced, casting a glare in all directions that would curdle milk. The salesman quickly gathered up his articles and quietly departed. A trip to the nearby equipment dealer for a part and its installation took no longer than a half hour and I was behind the wheel of the Massey again.

In mid-afternoon I drank iced tea again, not for refreshment, but to stay awake. The breeze from the tractor window was hot and slapped my dry, dust-covered face. My hands and fingernails were brown from gripping the steering wheel and making adjustments on the machinery. My shoes felt tight and my back sought relief from the tractor seat. The earplugs hurt my ears and my scalp itched. My nose was dry and crusty. My eyes strained past the glaring sun through the dusty rear window as I watched the wagon fill up once again. My underpants wedged.

Neighbors, friends, and tourists passed by the farm. The tourists often stopped beside the road and watched me work. They smiled. I waved to them. Of course they smiled. They were on vacation — on their way to park their camping trailer at a campground, to go for a swim, to eat at a restaurant or to see a play in Camden.

Young couples went by in pickup trucks, looking like one driver with two heads. I waved to them and wished them a pleasant evening. Stock cars on trailers rolled by on their way to Unity Raceway for the Saturday night races. I knew I would hear them go back by again at 11:30 that night, if I was in my bed by then.

Haylage fell on the ground from the front of the already-full wagon when I realized I hadn't been paying attention and had gone a few hundred feet farther than necessary.

I stopped the tractor. No truck had returned to the field, so I leaned back on the seat and closed my eyes. I don't know how much time had passed when Travis's truck horn jolted me from a sound sleep. "The belt on the blower broke and we replaced it," he shouted. Yes, I thought, another charge slip for the boot box already full of bills.

Henry, our plump, square-faced, eleven-year-old neighbor, was riding with Kyle when he returned for another load. Henry was curious about everything, especially machinery. When we did field work, he stood beside the road or in the field, watching, hoping someone would ask him to ride. Kyle had picked him up and would explain in great detail the activities of the day. Henry looked happy. The haylage was drier and slid easily into the truck as a cloud of dust billowed up from the sides of the wagon. As they drove away, I thought: there goes three more days of feed for fifty-five cows and forty heifers.

By this time, it must have been six o'clock. The cows were filing down the lane to the back pasture after milking. Lydia wasn't the first one out into the pasture, but she was the first one to lie down. I recognized her from a distance: her markings, her udder, her stride. I knew every cow at a glance. Like people, each cow had a distinct appearance and personality; some were pleasant, some grumpy, some relaxed, some nervous, some pretty, some common looking, some productive, some lazy. Lydia, at thirteen years, was the queen of our herd. She was a no-nonsense plodder who cranked out with ease 30,000 pounds (or roughly 3,750 gallons) of milk during one lactation. (A typical lactation lasts ten months, and an average cow gives 15,000 pounds.) Lydia ate during the entire milking period and saved her resting time for outside on the soft pasture. The younger cows went about grazing for the rest of the daylight hours. Cows eat the most at that time of day. They spend the dark and cool hours resting, chewing cud, and making milk. Because there was no shade in the pastures, the cows remained inside the barn during summer days to eat haylage. The barn was cool, and with the doors and windows open and a floor fan blowing, there was plenty of ventilation.

As the sun sank lower, I moved to the long field. The end was in sight, but the windrows now looked twice as big because of the shadows cast by the setting sun. Hazy clouds returned to the night sky and the air was cool. From the long field I could see only the top of the blue silo. I was not tired anymore.

Ron came to the field with two passengers in our pickup truck. Our friends, Gordon and Merrily Brown from Vermont, had come to pick up a bull calf that they would raise and use for a herd sire. Merrily joined me in the cab of the tractor and we chatted about books, quilting, family, and farming. She didn't do tractor work on their farm, but knew the process. Her presence kept me alert. It was now dark save for the tractor lights and the red sunset behind the White Mountains to the west.

"How many loads have you chopped?" Merrily asked as the chopper grabbed the last scraps in the middle of the field.

"This makes forty-four, a new record," I said. "Every load is three days' feed, and today we put in enough feed for a hundred and thirty-two days."

"That's what I call a day's work!" Merrily exclaimed.

It was ten o'clock when we finally sat down to eat supper. It was Karen's first time baking beans, and I had neglected to tell her not to stir them as they cooked all day, so they were a bit mushy. But who cared? What a treat to have a meal set before me after fifteen hours of work. Forty-four loads. Our best yet. A record day.

THE COWS ARE OUT!

TWENTY-NINE

Dreams and Sadness

After graduating from college in the mid-1980s, Kyle and his wife, Karen, decided to pursue their own dream and make agriculture their career — they returned home to Craneland Farm with us. I looked forward to their return because Kyle was interested in taking over the bookkeeping and I needed a break from that. There were certain other jobs on the farm that I vowed I'd never do again once Kyle returned and Karen joined him. Karen grew up on Long Island, New York, and had never even been close to a cow until her first visit to Craneland Farm when she was a college freshman. Regardless, her enthusiasm grew with each visit during college vacations and her summers working by Kyle's side. She joined us full-time on the farm after she graduated from college a year after Kyle. She and Kyle were married in the fall of 1986. Karen learned to milk and took over that responsibility. We were an official two-generation farm.

Although Kyle did take over most of the bookkeeping, there really was not much other relief. In fact, the workload actually seemed to increase because we had to raise more crops and milk more cows to earn enough income to support two families. After Kyle and Karen joined us, the milking herd increased to seventy-five, with a goal of having sixty cows producing milk at all times. If you counted calves, we might have well over one hundred animals at any given time. In comparison, when we bought the farm in 1966, we milked twenty-five cows. In the 1970s, we milked about forty, and in the early 1980s, we milked about fifty. And as always, farming remained a twenty-four-hour-a-day job — something that even after two decades I never really adjusted to. I just seemed to get more tired.

Ron and I expected that Kyle would return home with new ideas about methods of farming that he had learned at college — and he did. We agreed that we would at least listen and allow him to try some of them. After all, four years of agricultural education should be worth something.

First, Kyle requested a computer to keep the farm's financial records and calculate grain rations for the cows. The word "computer" wasn't even in our vocabulary. I told Kyle that our ledger method of bookkeeping had worked quite well for twenty years, so why change? Ron already had his own formula for figuring grain rations, and the cows had produced well on that formula. I wondered if I could learn to use a computer. Ron's fingers had always been too wide to even type. I resisted change, especially if it meant signing on the dotted line, so I also told Kyle that computers were too expensive. Besides, when would we find time to use one?

Kyle took every opportunity to argue in favor of buying a computer. We managed to put him off for a year, but his arguments seemed valid enough (he convinced me that I needed one to write my stories), so we gave in. Of course, all of Kyle's arguments in support of a computer turned out to be correct. Ron never placed his fingers on the keys, but he didn't hesitate to

An aerial view of Craneland Farm. The main house with attached shed and garage faces Route 220. Above the house is the workshop and dry cow barn. Behind the house is the milking barn, and directly beside that are the silos.

ask Kyle to print out a monthly cash flow statement or to calculate a new list of grain rations. I was grateful for my one, small piece of the computer — the word processor. My old typewriter, the one my father had bought for twenty-five dollars at a local pawnshop in Caribou after I was accepted at the University of Maine, was retired to the attic.

We actually tried many of Kyle's new ideas during his first three years with us. Some worked and some didn't. One summer our first crop of hay had been chopped into haylage and stored in our silo. The weather had been damp and humid. Since haylage can be harvested at about 50 percent moisture, the weather didn't hamper the harvest. Second-crop hay is a different story. It contains clover and other legumes, which make it heavier and harder to dry. To provide a variety of forage for the cows, we

Travis and me on his Harley-Davidson.

preferred to bale the second crop of hay. Because haylage need not be as dry to store as hay, Ron suggested adapting to the humid, showery weather by putting up more haylage and less baled hay. Kyle wanted to try something new that he had read about in dairy publications. As the hay was mowed, it would be sprayed with a solution of water and potassium carbonate. The soap-like solution strips the natural, waxy coating from the stems of the legumes, allowing them to dry quicker. I couldn't understand how spraying a wet solution on hay could possibly help it dry quicker, but I'd heard only part of the conversation as Kyle and Ron discussed it for several days. I didn't take them seriously until Kyle announced he was going to The County to buy the tanks and supplies necessary to apply the solution. He tried to convince me that the new method would work, but I adopted a wait-and-see attitude.

Ron and Kyle worked for several days and evenings installing the tank on the front of the tractor and connecting hoses to the spray bar on the mower. Then they placed another tank on the pickup truck for hauling water to refill the spray tank. After the weatherman predicted three days of sunny, humid weather, Kyle, with the new equipment in place, chose the thickest field of alfalfa and clover to mow. Even with ideal weather conditions, three days would be a minimum amount of

Kyle at Craneland Farm in the late 1980s.

Karen, Kyle's wife, in the mid-1980s. This heifer, Heather, was a college graduation gift from her parents.

time to make second-crop hay. The next day I tedded, and the third day Ron asked me to rake and bale the field of hay. The sky was overcast and showers were predicted for late afternoon. As I raked, a slight breeze moved through the windrows, but I doubted the hay was ready to bale. After adjusting the baler to make the loosest possible bales, I began. After a few trips around the field, I stopped to check the weight of the bales. They seemed light enough, so I tightened the setting on the baler to make them heavier and filled three trailers. After I finished baling and returned to the farm, it began to rain. We covered the full trailers with canvas. It was milking time, and when I walked into the barn, Kyle had fed out some of the freshly baled hay. The cows were devouring the leafy, green biscuits.

"Kyle," I said, "I know I'm a drag on progress and doubted that spraying would help dry the hay faster, but seeing is believing. I have to admit that you were right again."

Unfortunately, along with new ideas from the second generation also came the rising costs of machinery, parts and maintenance, supplies, labor, grain, fuel, electricity, veterinary care and medicines, bedding and taxes. Making ends meet had grown increasingly difficult.

Kyle and Karen shared the dream Ron and I had when we were just starting out — to live and work on the farm and raise their children in the safe, healthy environment of a rural community. Kyle's first choice was to farm, and he was great at it. He had wanted to farm since he was three. But ultimately, his family had to come first. He and Karen agonized over their situation. Should they just stick it out? Should they abandon their dream for security? By the early to mid-1990s, when Kyle still couldn't find the financial security he needed for his growing family after a decade of hard work, both he and Karen left Craneland Farm and reluctantly pursued other careers.

I will simply say this: It is sad that farmers can't earn enough from the sale of their product to help pass the family farm on to the next generation.

THE COWS ARE OUT!

THIRTY

A Man and His Work

The sun was warm on my legs, but the air on my face felt cool in the shade of the tractor canopy as I circled the outside of the field and mowed a second crop of hay under a clear blue September sky. The second-crop hay was more sparse than the first crop, but it was greener and lush with clover, making it harder to dry. And how the cows loved it! I was sure Mother Nature had her reasons, but I wondered — wouldn't it be better to have those long days in July, August and September instead of April, May and June? Then the second-crop hay would dry faster.

I had slept solidly the previous night, after mowing until dark — until butterflies had hovered over the small section of standing hay in the middle of the field; until crickets had sung and moths had taken nosedives; until the copper of sunset had flashed through the birches in the west. Until the full moon had risen in the east over the tips of evergreens.

Along the outside windrow, right along the edge of the woods, were the unmistakable signs of the approaching fall. Already there were patches of red and orange leaves. Goldenrod and ragweed had started to blossom. I ducked overhanging tree branches at the edge of the field. Apples drummed the top of the tractor canopy. Grass was tramped beneath a tree where apples had fallen and deer had feasted upon them. My nostrils flared at the pungent smell of the remaining half-rotten apples. Rusty ferns and raspberry bushes were dry and drooping. Birds would return to eat the ripest, dark red chokecherries. Mother Nature had even started to fold the Queen Anne's lace.

After mowing several windrows, I settled into the dull roar of the tractor and the steady whirr of this incredible new mowing machine. It seemed to float over the field and drift over bumps in comparison to our old one.

Ron had promised to climb Mount Katahdin with me right after the second crop was in, so I was wearing my new hiking shoes to break them in. I looked forward to climbing the mountain in the crisp fall air when the leaves were showing color.

Clover blossoms had dried into brown balls and grasshoppers leapt from under them. I was relieved that the birds had already hatched their babies and no longer had nests hidden in the hay. A dragonfly flitted along beside me before darting in front of the tractor.

I mowed around an old dug well that marks the location of a self-sufficient farm of many years ago. The well had been covered with planks and logs and was surrounded by weeds and goldenrod. It was one remnant of five small farms that had been bought during the 1940s and combined into one larger farm. We had rented one hundred acres of it for fifteen years.

I didn't know the time but I felt hungry, so I stopped the mower and drove the pickup to a nearby field where Ron was baling hay. We ate a picnic lunch in the shade on the edge of the field. I knew it would be the last time we would picnic at that spot because the land would not be available for us to rent the

Ron replacing a tine on the pinwheel hay rake, 1989. Dairy farming was all Ron ever really wanted to do.

next year. With our new land on Beaver Hill coming into full production that year, we hoped we could make up for the loss of the rented acreage. I looked around sadly, memorizing the shape of the field, the view, and past picnics in that beautiful place.

There was just so much beauty on Knox Ridge; so much to love. It was this beauty that kept me energized and revitalized me when the stress of unpaid bills and the endless work threatened to overwhelm me. It was now the mid-1980s, we were roughly two decades into farming, and at times the work seemed to grow increasingly tiresome to me. As I aged and grew more weary, I needed to cherish these beautiful days. I needed the rejuvenation they provided, especially now that Jud was gone.

I had asked Ron to quit farming once. It was in the early 1970s after Ron's brother, Bob, and his wife, Marty, had come home from the Air Force to farm with us. Bob, Marty, and their newborn daughter, Kimberly, lived with us while they looked for their own place to live. After six years of not having enough hired help and working with our noses to the grindstone, it was wonderful to have someone to share in the work.

As soon as Bob and his family arrived, he and Ron went to work in our woods cutting logs and hauling them out with our neighbor's son, Nathan, at the reins of their workhorse, Reny. Ron and Bob designed a forty-by-sixty-foot barn ell so that we could milk enough cows to support two families. Ron and Bob hauled the harvested logs to a nearby mill to saw. Then, with the help of Keith Overlock, a local carpenter, they worked long days, nights, and weekends to complete the barn ell. Marty and I shingled the northwest side of the addition in January.

While the men worked on the new barn, Marty and I took turns helping with barn chores and caring for baby Kimberly. We also froze beans and corn and made pickles and applesauce for the winter. She had been a city girl and this kind of work was all new to her. I think it helped take her mind off the fact that she hadn't seen much of Bob since they'd come to the farm.

"Do you think we'll eat all this corn?" Marty asked as we filled bags of corn for the freezer.

"Wait until February and you'll see," I replied.

One night at supper, Bob asked his brother, "Have you always worked this hard?"

"Pretty much," Ron replied. "There's so much to do when you first start out farming."

"You've been here six years," Bob reminded him. "That's not just starting out."

"And I have a lot more to do before I feel that I can slack off," Ron replied.

"I can't do it," Bob said. "I can't work twenty-four hours a day. And besides that, the cows all look alike to me. I've been here for six months and I still don't know one from the other. I don't even *like* cows."

Looking back, Ron has said that he worked Bob too hard, that he should have done it differently.

By Christmas, Bob and Marty found a new place to live and Bob took a different job. Ron, the boys and I assumed our old and now additional chores again with very few breaks.

As we ate supper a short time later, weariness overwhelmed me. I tried to pay attention as the boys chattered about their friends and school. I stared at my plate and pushed my fork into the soft, warm mashed potatoes. My eyes closed.

"Are you nodding off?" Ron asked.

"Oh," I said, blinking, "I guess I was. I'm tired and not very hungry."

After I had heard the boys' prayers and tucked them in for the night, I went into the playroom and turned off the TV.

"What are you doing?" Ron asked.

"We need to talk," I said, sitting next to him on the couch. "Let's sell the farm."

"What are you saying?" Ron asked, rising and sitting up to face me.

I said again, "Let's sell the farm. I can't take it anymore. Work, work, work. It's chores in the morning, rush into the house, get the boys off to school, and finish chores. When they get home from school, it's back to the barn for more chores. Then it's back into the house to fix supper and fall into bed; that is, if I don't fall asleep at the supper table first. I just can't do it anymore."

"I didn't realize you felt that way. Everything has been going pretty well lately," Ron remarked.

"Maybe for you, but not for me. I was doing great when Bob and Marty were here. Even though we worked hard building the new barn, at least there was a break from chores. When they left, we were right back where we were before, with more to do. And I can't see any relief. It's not that I don't like the farm — I do. I love living here. I love bringing up the boys here. I love most everything about it, but once in a while I need a break from the incessant chores."

"I had no idea you were unhappy. Why didn't you tell me before?"

"I thought I could do it because you do it. I thought there was something wrong with me because I couldn't keep up with you. Now I know that *no one* can keep up with you — not I, nor your brother or anyone else. I can't see any other way but to sell the farm. I can't enjoy life if all I do is work."

"Please don't ask me to sell the farm," Ron pleaded. "I can't do that. I won't do that. We can make some changes — maybe hire someone so that you don't have to work so hard. Then you'd have more time for other things. We'll milk a few more cows to pay a hired person like we had planned when Bob was here. Besides, what else would I do if I didn't farm?"

"You could teach school," I said. "You could work for someone else so that you'd have time off."

"But I don't want to teach school. I'd be a lousy teacher. And I don't want to work for someone else. I like working for myself. I don't want to do anything else. Don't you understand? All I've ever wanted is to farm."

He was right, of course; farming is all he ever wanted to do — and he was great at it. And despite my request that night,

206

we spent many more wonderful years at Craneland Farm. Indeed, farming was also part of my dream, and I was able to live it amongst the fields and under the blue sky along Knox Ridge. But unlike Ron, farming was not my only dream.

Times change. Seasons change. And so, sometimes, do dreams.

The Cows are Out!

Dusk:

An Epilogue

I loved Craneland Farm, but I left it for good in 1989. Ron and I divorced eighteen months later. When we began farming in 1966, I told Ron that I would give it twenty years. If after that I didn't feel financially secure, I wanted to seek alternatives. For more than twenty years we farmed with the help of our two growing sons, hoping that someday one or both of them would want to continue in the profession. It didn't take long for me to realize that my dream of owning the farm free and clear would never become a reality. Security never came — only exhaustion. And the boys never took over the farm.

My granddaughter, Karlee, and me at Bailey Island in the fall of 2000.

Kyle and Travis have stayed close to their farming roots, but neither remained in dairy farming. After several years of farming with Ron, both Kyle and Karen changed careers in 1992 because the farm could not provide enough financial security for their growing family. Kyle is now the principal of Searsport District Middle School and Karen works as a proofreader for Thorndike Press. They live two miles from Craneland Farm with their three children, Kevin, Kody, and Karlee.

Travis, who attended the University of Maine and took the agricultural mechanization technology course, worked on the farm with his father for a year and still helps with machinery maintenance when needed. But his main job now is working with his Uncle Bob in the insulation business. He lives one mile from the farm with his girlfriend Rhonda Gardiner, two pit bulls, Harley and Stroker, and her German shepherd, Amen.

Kyle and Travis as they looked back when it all started in 1966.

Danny, the local boy who lived with us off and on for several years, lives in Hamburg. He was able to trace his Sicilian roots, became an Italian citizen and works in Germany.

My beloved horse Jud was with us for twelve years on the farm. In the early 1980s, he was diagnosed with a twisted intestine and had to be put down. He is buried in the back pasture.

Our prized cow, Lydia, lived to be nineteen years old. She produced record amounts of milk and many offspring, both naturally and by embryo transfer. There was no beef truck ride for her. She also is buried in the back pasture.

This sign, featuring our prized cow Lydia hung outside at Craneland Farm for many years.

Kay Raven, that blond, blue-eyed girl who was in my third-grade class in 1970 and then worked at Craneland Farm for a decade, realized her dream of marrying a dairy farmer and having children. She and her husband, Larry Seehafer, continue to dairy farm in Marathon, Wisconsin, where they homeschool their six children.

Ron continues to live and work at Craneland Farm and is joined part-time by our young grandsons, Kevin and Kody. They are the third generation of our family to help in the business.

As for me, I work as a manager at the Maine Coast Book Shop & Café in Damariscotta, a far cry from the farm on Knox Ridge. I think of the farm every day, though, and occasionally, it seems like it would be easier to milk the cows.

Looking back, I'm glad I farmed. It helped make me who I am today. I couldn't do my present job as well had I not learned the work ethic that started in the potato fields of Aroostook County and was fully developed on Knox Ridge. And, Ron and

I gave our sons the gift of growing up in a world of animals and nature — a gift that I believe provided the base that has made them productive citizens.

On the other hand, farming featured, in my mind, crushing demands. In addition to the overwhelming twenty-four-hour-a-day, seven-day-a-week demands of dairy farming, my biggest frustration with farming was the lack of financial reward for the amount of work required. Common refrains heard on farms across the nation are: "If I just work harder, then I'll be able to pay those bills," and, "Next year will be better, you'll see." For the most part, these comments are just wishful thinking at best, complete denial at worst.

You may think you are your own boss on a dairy farm, but you are not. You cannot control the price you receive for your product. You exist at the mercy of milk prices, the cost of fuel to truck it to the dairy (a farmer pays per mile, per hundredweight of milk), the cost of grain and equipment, and the repairs necessary to get the job done. Consider this: When we bought our farm in 1966 for $50,000, financial institutions questioned whether a mid-sized dairy herd could support the escalating costs. By 1986, a tractor alone cost $75,000. Ultimately, I found that I needed more financial security. I needed to be able to pay the bills. At Craneland Farm, I wasn't able to do that. The reality was that I wasn't able to work any harder. And, frankly, I was simply exhausted. Twenty-three years is a long time.

Unquestionably, there are aspects of farming that I miss terribly. I treasure the unforgettable memories of family dinners and picnics, of working together for common goals, and of sunrises and sunsets on The Ridge. I loved the taste of our own fresh milk, meat, eggs and vegetables, the feel of Brigette's huge

A painting of Craneland Farm under gathering skies by Linden Frederick.

head pushing up under my hand, the smell of new-mown hay, the warm sun on my bare skin and the feel of Hetty's leather show halter in my hand.

Fortunately, I can bring to consciousness the feeling of freedom and of being one with my spirited horse, Jud, at any time.

To this day, I still stir at five in the morning — chore time — and often think back on the beautiful simplicity of my old job — carrying pails of milk to waiting calves. Today, however, I can lay my head back on the pillow and doze for another hour.

In the end, the bottom line is this: It was my dream, starting as a little girl in Aroostook County, to own my own horse, to ride him bareback across my own fields, and to enjoy the pure freedom of the life I chose.

And I did.

THE COWS ARE OUT!

About the Author

Trudy Chambers Price was born in Island Falls, Maine, and grew up in the Aroostook County town of Caribou. Her family has lived in The County for more than five generations. She was one of three children and like most County youths, earned money picking potatoes, starting at the age of ten and working for twenty-five cents a barrel.

Trudy graduated from Caribou High School in 1958, and from the University of Maine at Orono in 1962 with a degree in psychology and a minor in elementary education. She helped pay her way through college working as a carhop at the Sesme in Caribou. She married Ron Price the day she graduated.

Photo by Dean L. Lunt

Trudy, 2003.

215

In 1966, she and Ron purchased a 150-acre dairy farm in Knox, Maine (about fifteen miles from Belfast), where the couple worked together for the next twenty-three years, while also raising their children, Kyle and Travis. During her time at Craneland Farm, she also spent two years teaching third grade at Mt. View Elementary School in Thorndike to help pay the farm bills. She also began to write about her experiences working full-time as a dairy farmer. *The Cows Are Out!* is the result of that effort, begun on a typewriter in her old farmhouse on Knox Ridge. Trudy now lives in Brunswick and works as a manager at the Maine Coast Book Shop & Café in Damariscotta. *The Cows Are Out!* is her first book.

Glossary

apportion: to divide and distribute grain in unequal shares according to a plan

bull: a fertile adult male bovine

bull proof: record of a bull's daughters, including their milk production and physical traits

calf: a newborn cow or bull

classification: a score assigned to a cow or bull by an official classifier from the particular breed association, such as Holstein-Friesian, based on the body conformation

colostrum: the first fluid, rich in protein, secreted by the cow's udder for several days after calving

cow: a mature female bovine

cud: a mouthful of previously swallowed food regurgitated from the first two chambers of a cow's stomach back to the mouth where it is chewed slowly for a second time

dam: a female parent of a calf

dry cow: a pregnant cow, not producing milk for a period (usually 2 months) before giving birth again

embryo transfer: the process of transplanting embryos from a donor cow to a recipient (surrogate), or the result of that action

forage:	(also called roughage) food for domestic animals (cows), including coarse substances such as hay, haylage and corn silage that is high in cellulose and other indigestible components
graining:	feeding grain to cattle; different amounts of grain are hand-fed based on milk production — the more milk a cow produces, the more grain she requires for proper nutrition
haylage:	chopped hay which is usually stored in a silo
heifer:	a young cow that has not borne a calf
Holstein:	a breed of large, black-and-white dairy cattle; also called Holstein-Friesian
Jersey:	a breed of small dairy cattle, often light red or fawn-colored; its milk has a high butterfat content
"making" hay:	getting the hay dry enough to bale and store away by tedding and raking
mastitis:	inflammation of the udder
mess:	(of fiddleheads or greens) a desirable amount picked to serve several people
pedigree:	the recorded ancestry, especially of purebred cattle, with official milk records, bull proofs, classification scores and often a photograph
registration:	identification and proof of the purebred cow or bull through application to the breed association
ringworm:	a contagious skin fungus, characterized by itching and the formation of ring-shaped discolored patches covered with scales
sire:	a male parent of a calf

stanchion:	a stall made of pipes or wood surrounding the cow with a method (chain/strap) of hitching her
"standing heat":	during the period of sexual excitement in cows, the point at which the female stands still when being ridden piggyback by another animal, artificially inseminated or while a bull inseminates her
steer:	a castrated male bovine
tedder/ted:	a machine pulled by a tractor that teds (spreads out) the hay from a windrow so that it dries faster
windrow:	a windrow of hay is a row of mowed hay raked together to dry before being baled; a windrow of haylage is a row of mowed, unraked hay that will be chopped into haylage

The Cows are Out!